United States General Accounting Office

GAO

Report to Congressional Requesters

I0411755

March 2004

INFORMATION SECURITY

Technologies to Secure Federal Systems

GAO

Accountability ★ Integrity ★ Reliability

GAO-04-467

March 2004

INFORMATION SECURITY

Technologies to Secure Federal Systems

Highlights of GAO-04-467, a report to Congressional Requesters

Why GAO Did This Study

Federal agencies rely extensively on computerized information systems and electronic data to carry out their missions. The security of these systems and data is essential to preventing data tampering, disruptions in critical operations, fraud, and inappropriate disclosure of sensitive information.

Congress and the executive branch have taken actions to address this challenge, such as enacting and implementing the Federal Information Security Management Act (FISMA). FISMA and other federal guidance discuss the need for specific technical controls to secure information systems. In order to meet the requirements of FISMA to effectively implement these technical controls, it is critical that federal agencies consider whether they have adequately implemented available cybersecurity technologies.

GAO was asked by the Chairmen of the House Committee on Government Reform and its Subcommittee on Technology, Information Policy, Intergovernmental Relations and the Census to identify commercially available, state-of-the-practice cybersecurity technologies that federal agencies can use to defend their computer systems against cyber attacks.

www.gao.gov/cgi-bin/getrpt?GAO-04-467.

To view the full product, including the scope and methodology, click on the link above. For more information, contact Robert F. Dacey at (202) 512-3317 or daceyr@gao.gov.

What GAO Found

Many cybersecurity technologies offered in today's marketplace can serve as safeguards and countermeasures to protect agencies' information technology infrastructures. To assist agencies in identifying and selecting such technologies, we have categorized specific technologies according to the control functionality they provide and described what the technologies do, how they work, and their reported effectiveness. The following table defines these five control categories:

Cybersecurity Control Categories	
Control category	Control functionality
Access controls	Restrict the ability of unknown or unauthorized users to view or use information, hosts, or networks.
System integrity	Ensures that a system and its data are not illicitly modified or corrupted by malicious code.
Cryptography	Includes encryption of data during transmission and when stored on a system. Encryption is the process of transforming ordinary data into code form so that the information is accessible only to those who are authorized to have access.
Audit and monitoring	Help administrators to perform investigations during and after a cyber attack.
Configuration management and assurance	Help administrators view and change the security settings on their hosts and networks, verify the correctness of security settings, and maintain operations in a secure fashion under conditions of duress.

Source: GAO analysis.

We identified 18 technologies that are available within these categories, including smart tokens—which establish users' identities through an integrated circuit chip in a portable device such as a smart card or a time-synchronized token—and security event correlation tools—which monitor and document actions on network devices and analyze the actions to determine if an attack is ongoing or has occurred.

The selection and effective implementation of cybersecurity technologies require adequate consideration of a number of key factors, including:

- implementing technologies through a layered, defense-in-depth strategy;
- considering the agency's unique information technology infrastructure when selecting technologies;
- utilizing results of independent testing when assessing the technologies' capabilities;
- training staff on the secure implementation and utilization of these technologies; and
- ensuring that the technologies are securely configured.

Contents

Letter   1

Cybersecurity Technologies Overview   1
Background   2
Effective Implementation of Commercially Available Technologies
    Can Mitigate Risks   9
Implementation Considerations Should Be Addressed   74

Appendix I   **Objective, Scope, and Methodology**   81

Appendix II   **Staff Acknowledgments**   83

Acknowledgments   83

Tables

Table 1: Cybersecurity Control Categories   2
Table 2: Cybersecurity Technology Control Categories and
    Technologies   12

Figures

Figure 1: Typical IT Infrastructure   10
Figure 2: A Typical Firewall Protecting Hosts on a Private Network
    from the Public Network   15
Figure 3: How a Web Filter Works   22
Figure 4: An Example of Fingerprint Recognition Technology Built
    into a Keyboard   27
Figure 5: An Example of Fingerprint Recognition Technology Built
    into a Mouse   27
Figure 6: A Desktop Iris Recognition System   28
Figure 7: Example of a Time-Synchronized Token   32
Figure 8: Example of a Challenge-Response Token   32
Figure 9: Encryption and Decryption with a Symmetric Algorithm   41
Figure 10: Encryption and Decryption with a Public Key Algorithm   42
Figure 11: Creating a Digital Signature   46
Figure 12: Verifying a Digital Signature   47
Figure 13: Illustration of a Typical VPN   48
Figure 14: Tunneling Establishes a Virtual Connection   50
Figure 15: Typical Operation of Security Event Correlation Tools   57

Figure 16: Typical Network Management Architecture 65
Figure 17: Example of a Vulnerability Scanner Screen 71
Figure 18: Layered Approach to Network Security 76

Abbreviations

CMIP	common management information protocol
COTS	commercial off-the-shelf
DHCP	dynamic host configuration protocol
DSL	digital subscriber line
FISMA	Federal Information Security Management Act
GISRA	Government Information Security Reform provisions
HTML	Hypertext Markup Language
ID	identification
IDS	intrusion detection system
IP	Internet protocol
IPS	intrusion prevention system
IPSec	Internet protocol security protocol
ISP	Internet service provider
IT	information technology
LAN	local area network
NAT	network address translation
NIAP	National Information Assurance Partnership
NIPC	National Infrastructure Protection Center
NIST	National Institute of Standards and Technology
NSA	National Security Agency
OMB	Office of Management and Budget
PC	personal computer
PIN	personal identification number
PKI	public key infrastructure
RADIUS	Remote Authentication Dial-In User Service
RAID	redundant array of independent disks
SNMP	simple network management protocol
SSL	Secure Sockets Layer
TACACS+	Terminal Access Controller Access System
TCP	transmission control protocol
UDP	user datagram protocol
VPN	virtual private network
WAN	wide area network
XML	Extensible Markup Language

United States General Accounting Office
Washington, DC 20548

March 9, 2004

The Honorable Tom Davis
Chairman, Committee on Government Reform
House of Representatives

The Honorable Adam Putnam
Chairman, Subcommittee on Technology, Information Policy,
    Intergovernmental Relations and the Census
Committee on Government Reform
House of Representatives

Federal agencies rely extensively on computerized information systems
and electronic data to carry out their missions. The security of these
systems and data is essential to preventing data tampering, disruptions in
critical operations, fraud, and inappropriate disclosure of sensitive
information. In accordance with your request, our objective was to
identify commercially available, state-of-the-practice cybersecurity
technologies that federal agencies can use to defend their computer
systems against cyber attacks.[1] We developed a catalog that lists these
technologies and describes them according to the functionality they
provide. The discussion of each technology is technical in nature and is
intended to assist agencies in identifying and selecting cybersecurity
technologies that can be deployed. Appendix I contains a detailed
description of our objective, scope, and methodology.

Cybersecurity Technologies Overview

There are many cybersecurity technologies offered in today's marketplace
that can serve as safeguards and countermeasures to protect agencies'
information technology (IT) infrastructures. We identify 18 technologies
and describe what they do, how they work, and their reported

---

[1]It is important to note that physical security and cybersecurity are intertwined, and both
are necessary to achieve overall security. Physical security typically involves protecting
any physical asset—from entire buildings to computer hardware—from physical attacks,
whereas cybersecurity usually focuses on protecting software and data from attacks that
are electronic in nature and that typically arrive over a data communication link.

GAO-04-467 Information Security

effectiveness. These technologies can be categorized by the control functionality they provide. Table 1 defines these control categories:

Table 1: Cybersecurity Control Categories

Control category	Control functionality
Access controls	Restrict the ability of unknown or unauthorized users to view or use information, hosts, or networks.
System integrity	Ensures that a system and its data are not illicitly modified or corrupted by malicious code.
Cryptography	Includes encryption of data during transmission and when stored on a system. Encryption is the process of transforming ordinary data into code form so that the information is accessible only to those who are authorized to have access.
Audit and monitoring	Help administrators to perform investigations during and after a cyber attack.
Configuration management and assurance	Help administrators view and change the security settings on their hosts and networks, verify the correctness of security settings, and maintain operations in a secure fashion under conditions of duress.

Source: GAO analysis.

The selection and effective implementation of cybersecurity technologies require adequate consideration of several key factors, including considering the agency's unique IT infrastructure and utilizing a layered, defense-in-depth strategy.

Background

Information security is an important consideration for any organization that depends on information systems to carry out its mission. The dramatic expansion in computer interconnectivity and the exponential increase in the use of the Internet are changing the way our government, the nation, and much of the world communicate and conduct business. However, without proper safeguards, the speed and accessibility that create the enormous benefits of the computer age may allow individuals and groups with malicious intentions to gain unauthorized access to systems and use this access to obtain sensitive information, commit fraud, disrupt operations, or launch attacks against other organizations' sites.

Experts agree that there has been a steady advance in the sophistication and effectiveness of attack technology. Intruders quickly develop attacks to exploit the vulnerabilities discovered in products, use these attacks to compromise computers, and share them with other attackers. In addition, they can combine these attacks with other forms of technology to develop programs that automatically scan a network for vulnerable systems, attack them, compromise them, and use them to spread the attack even further. These attack tools have become readily available, and can be easily downloaded from the Internet and, with a simple "point and click," used to launch an attack.

Government officials are concerned about attacks from individuals and groups with malicious intent, such as crime, terrorism, foreign intelligence gathering, and acts of war. According to the Federal Bureau of Investigation, terrorists, transnational criminals, and intelligence services are quickly becoming aware of and using information exploitation tools such as computer viruses, Trojan horses, worms, logic bombs, and eavesdropping sniffers that can destroy, intercept, degrade the integrity of, or deny access to data.[2] In addition, the disgruntled organization insider is a significant threat, since such individuals often have knowledge that allows them to gain unrestricted access and inflict damage or steal assets without possessing a great deal of knowledge about computer intrusions. As greater amounts of money and more sensitive economic and commercial information are exchanged electronically, and as the nation's defense and intelligence communities increasingly rely on standardized information technology, the likelihood increases that information attacks will threaten vital national interests.

According to the National Security Agency (NSA), foreign governments already have or are developing computer attack capabilities, and potential adversaries are developing a body of knowledge about U.S. systems and about methods to attack these systems. In his February 2002 statement before the Senate Select Committee on Intelligence, the Director of Central Intelligence discussed the possibility of a cyber warfare attack by

---

[2] *Virus:* a program that "infects" computer files, usually executable programs, by inserting a copy of itself into the file. These copies are usually executed when the infected file is loaded into memory, allowing the virus to infect other files. Unlike the computer worm, a virus requires human involvement (usually unwitting) to propagate. *Trojan horse:* a computer program that conceals harmful code. A Trojan horse usually masquerades as a useful program that a user would wish to execute. *Worm:* an independent computer program that reproduces by copying itself from one system to another across a network. Unlike computer viruses, worms do not require human involvement to propagate. *Logic bomb:* in programming, a form of sabotage in which a programmer inserts code that causes the program to perform a destructive action when some triggering event, such as termination of the programmer's employment, occurs. *Sniffer:* synonymous with packet sniffer. A program that intercepts routed data and examines each packet in search of specified information, such as passwords transmitted in clear text.

terrorists.[3] He stated that the September 11, 2001, attacks demonstrated the nation's dependence on critical infrastructure systems that rely on electronic and computer networks. He noted that attacks of this nature would become an increasingly viable option for terrorists as they and other foreign adversaries become more familiar with these targets and the technologies required to attack them.

In 2003, the Federal Computer Incident Response Center documented 1,433,916 cybersecurity incidents related to systems at federal agencies and departments—compared with 489,890 incidents in 2002.[4] This dramatic increase may be related to the military actions taken by the United States against Iraq in 2003. According to the Department of Homeland Security's National Infrastructure Protection Center (NIPC), illegal cyber activity often escalates during a time of increased international tension. This kind of activity can be state sponsored or encouraged and can come from domestic organizations or individuals acting independently or from sympathetic entities around the world who view their actions as a form of political activism. In February 2003, NIPC issued an advisory on the increase in global hacking activities as a result of the growing tensions between the United States and Iraq, warning computer users and system administrators of the potential for increased cyber disruption. NIPC advised owners and operators of computers and networked systems to limit potential problems by using security best practices.[5]

Since September 1996, we have reported that poor information security is a widespread problem in the federal government with potentially devastating consequences.[6] We have identified information security as a government-wide high-risk issue in reports to Congress since 1997—most

---

[3]Testimony of George J. Tenet, Director of Central Intelligence, before the Senate Select Committee on Intelligence, Feb. 6, 2002.

[4]The Federal Computer Incident Response Center tracks a variety of incident types such as root compromise, user compromise, denial of service, malicious code, Web site defacement, misuse of resources, and reconnaissance activity.

[5]U.S. Department of Homeland Security, *Encourages Heightened Cyber Security as Iraq-U.S. Tensions Increase*, Advisory 03-002 (February 11, 2003).

[6]U.S. General Accounting Office, *Information Security: Opportunities for Improved OMB Oversight of Agency Practices*, GAO/AIMD-96-110 (Washington, D.C.: September 24, 1996).

recently in January 2003.[7] Although agencies have taken steps to redesign and strengthen their information system security programs, our analyses of major federal agencies have shown that federal systems have not been adequately protected from computer-based threats, even though these systems process, store, and transmit enormous amounts of sensitive data and are indispensable to many agencies' operations. For the past several years, we have analyzed audit results for 24 of the largest federal agencies and we have found that all 24 had significant information security weaknesses.[8]

Federal Legislation Emphasizes Computer Security

Concerned with accounts of attacks on systems via the Internet and reports of significant weaknesses in federal computer systems that make them vulnerable to attack, in October 2000 Congress passed and the President signed into law Government Information Security Reform provisions (commonly known as GISRA).[9] To strengthen information security practices throughout the federal government, GISRA established information security program, evaluation, and reporting requirements for federal agencies.

In December 2002, the Federal Information Security Management Act (FISMA), enacted as Title III of the E-Government Act of 2002, permanently authorized and strengthened GISRA requirements.[10] FISMA requires each agency to develop, document, and implement an agencywide

---

[7]U.S. General Accounting Office, *High-Risk Series: Protecting Information Systems Supporting the Federal Government and the Nation's Critical Infrastructures*, GAO-03-121 (Washington, D.C.: January 2003).

[8]U.S. General Accounting Office, *Information Security: Serious Weaknesses Place Critical Federal Operations and Assets at Risk*, GAO/AIMD-98-92 (Washington, D.C.: September 23, 1998); *Information Security: Serious and Widespread Weaknesses Persist at Federal Agencies* GAO/AIMD-00-295 (Washington, D.C.: September 6, 2000); *Computer Security: Improvements Needed to Reduce Risk to Critical Federal Operations and Assets*, GAO-02-231T (Washington, D.C.: Nov. 9, 2001); *Computer Security: Progress Made, but Critical Federal Operations and Assets Remain at Risk*, GAO-02-303T (Washington, D.C.: November 19, 2002); and *Information Security: Progress Made, but Challenges Remain to Protect Federal Systems and the Nation's Critical Infrastructures*, GAO-03-564T (Washington, D.C.: April 8, 2003).

[9]Government Information Security Reform, Title X, Subtitle G, Floyd D. Spence National Defense Authorization Act for Fiscal Year 2001, P.L. 106-398, October 30, 2000.

[10]Federal Information Security Management Act of 2002, Title III, E-Government Act of 2002, P.L. 107-347, December 17, 2002. This act superseded an earlier version of FISMA that was enacted as Title X of the Homeland Security Act of 2002.

information security program to provide information security for the information and systems that support the operations and assets of the agency, using a risk-based approach to information security management. In addition, FISMA requires the National Institute of Standards and Technology (NIST) to develop risk-based minimum information security standards for systems other than those dealing with national security. The Cyber Security Research and Development Act requires NIST to develop, and revise as necessary, checklists providing suggested configurations that minimize the security risks associated with each computer hardware or software system that is, or is likely to become, widely used within the federal government.[11]

A Comprehensive Information Security Management Program Is Essential

FISMA recognized that the underlying cause for the majority of security problems in federal agencies is the lack of an effective information security management program. No matter how sophisticated technology becomes, it will never solve management issues. Furthermore, because of the vast differences in types of federal systems and the variety of risks associated with each of them, there is no single approach to security that will be effective for all systems. Therefore, following basic risk management steps is fundamental to determining security priorities and implementing appropriate solutions.

Our May 1998 study of security management best practices determined that a comprehensive information security management program is essential to ensuring that information system controls work effectively on a continuing basis.[12] The effective implementation of appropriate, properly designed security controls is an essential element for ensuring the confidentiality, integrity, and availability of the information that is transmitted, processed, and stored on agencies' IT infrastructures. Weak security controls can expose information to an increased risk of unauthorized access, use, disclosure, disruption, modification, and destruction.

An effective program should establish a framework and a continuing cycle of activity for assessing risk, developing and implementing effective security procedures, and monitoring the effectiveness of these procedures.

---

[11]Cyber Security Research and Development Act, P.L. 107-305, November 27, 2002.

[12]U.S. General Accounting Office, *Information Security Management: Learning from Leading Organizations*, GAO/AIMD-98-68 (Washington, D.C.: May 1, 1998).

The recently enacted FISMA, consistent with our study, describes certain key elements of a comprehensive information security management program. These elements include

- a senior agency information security officer with the mission and resources to ensure FISMA compliance;
- periodic assessments of the risk and magnitude of the harm that could result from the unauthorized access, use, disclosure, disruption, modification, or destruction of information and information systems;

- policies and procedures that (1) are based on risk assessments, (2) cost-effectively reduce risks, (3) ensure that information security is addressed throughout the life cycle of each system, and (4) ensure compliance with applicable requirements;

- security awareness training to inform personnel, including contactors and other users of information systems, of information security risks and their responsibilities in complying with agency policies and procedures; and

- at least annual testing and evaluation of the effectiveness of information security policies, procedures, and practices relating to management, operational, and technical controls of every major information system that is identified in agencies' inventories.

Federal Government Is Taking Actions to Implement FISMA and Improve Information Security

The Office of Management and Budget (OMB) and NIST have taken a number of actions to implement FISMA and improve information security. Preceding FISMA, OMB issued Circular A-130, *Management of Federal Resources*, Appendix III, "Security of Federal Information Resources," which establishes a minimum set of controls that agencies must include in their information security programs. NIST continues to publish guidance for improving information security, in addition to developing the minimum standards required by FISMA.[13] The administration has undertaken other important actions to improve information security, such as integrating information security into the President's Management Agenda Scorecard and issuing annual reports on the implementation of GISRA (and now FISMA) that analyzed federal government's information security challenges.

---

[13]See NIST's FISMA Implementation Project Web site at http://csrc.ncsl.nist.gov/sec-cert/.

In addition, OMB has provided annual guidance to agencies on how to implement GISRA and FISMA.[14] For the last 2 years, this guidance has instructed agencies to use NIST Special Publication 800-26, *Security Self-Assessment Guide for Information Technology Systems*, to conduct their annual reviews. This guide builds on the *Federal IT Security Assessment Framework,* which NIST developed for the Federal Chief Information Officer Council. The framework includes guidelines for assessing agencies' implementations of specific technical controls such as antivirus software, technologies to ensure data integrity, intrusion detection tools, firewalls, and audit and monitoring tools. In the meantime, NIST, as required by FISMA, has been working to develop specific cybersecurity standards and guidelines for federal information systems, including

- standards to be used by all federal agencies to categorize all information and information systems based on the objective of providing appropriate levels of information security according to a range of risk levels;

- guidelines recommending the types of information and information systems to include in each category; and

- minimum information security requirements for information and information systems in each category.

NIST issued the first of these required documents, *Standards for Security Categorization of Federal Information and Information Systems,* Federal Information Processing Standards Publication 199 (commonly referred to as FIPS 199) in December 2003. Drafts of additional standards and guidelines were recently released for public comment.[15]

FIPS 199 established three levels of potential impact of cyber attacks on organizations or individuals—low, moderate, and high—and categorized information and information systems with respect to three security

---

[14]See Office of Management and Budget, *Memorandum for Heads of Executive Departments and Agencies,* M-03-19 (Washington, D.C.: August 6, 2003) for OMB's 2003 FISMA reporting guidance.

[15]National Institute of Standards and Technology, *Guide for Mapping Types of Information and Information Systems to Security Categories,* NIST Special Publication 800-60, Initial Public Draft, Version 1.0 (December 2003) and National Institute of Standards and Technology, *Recommended Security Controls for Federal Information Systems,* NIST Special Publication 800-53, Initial Public Draft, Version 1.0 (October 2003).

objectives—confidentiality, integrity, and availability.[16] NIST recommends that three general classes of security controls be employed—management, operational, and technical—to support these security objectives. The number and type of controls should be commensurate with the level of potential impact. Technical controls recommended by NIST should address identification and authentication, logical access control, accountability, and system communications protection.

Effective Implementation of Commercially Available Technologies Can Mitigate Risks

To fulfill the requirements of FISMA and effectively implement the technical controls discussed above, it is critical that federal agencies consider whether they have adequately implemented available technologies. A plethora of cybersecurity technologies offered in today's marketplace can serve as safeguards and countermeasures to protect agencies' IT infrastructures. To assist agencies in identifying and considering the need to further implement such technologies, this document provides a structured discussion of commercially available, state-of-the-practice cybersecurity technologies that federal agencies can use to secure their computer systems. It also discusses cybersecurity implementation considerations.

Typically, agencies' infrastructures are built upon multiple hosts, including desktop personal computers (PCs), servers, and mainframes. Data communications links and network devices such as routers, hubs, and switches enable the hosts to communicate with one another through local area networks (LANs) within agencies. Wide area networks (WANs) connect LANs at different geographical locations. Moreover, agencies are typically connected to the Internet—the worldwide collection of networks, operated by some 10,000 Internet service providers (ISP). An example of a typical IT infrastructure is illustrated in figure 1.

---

[16]Confidentiality refers to preserving authorized restrictions on information access and disclosure, including the means for protecting personal privacy and proprietary information. Integrity refers to guarding against improper modification or destruction of information, including ensuring information nonrepudiation and authenticity. Availability refers to ensuring timely and reliable access to and use of information.

Figure 1: Typical IT Infrastructure

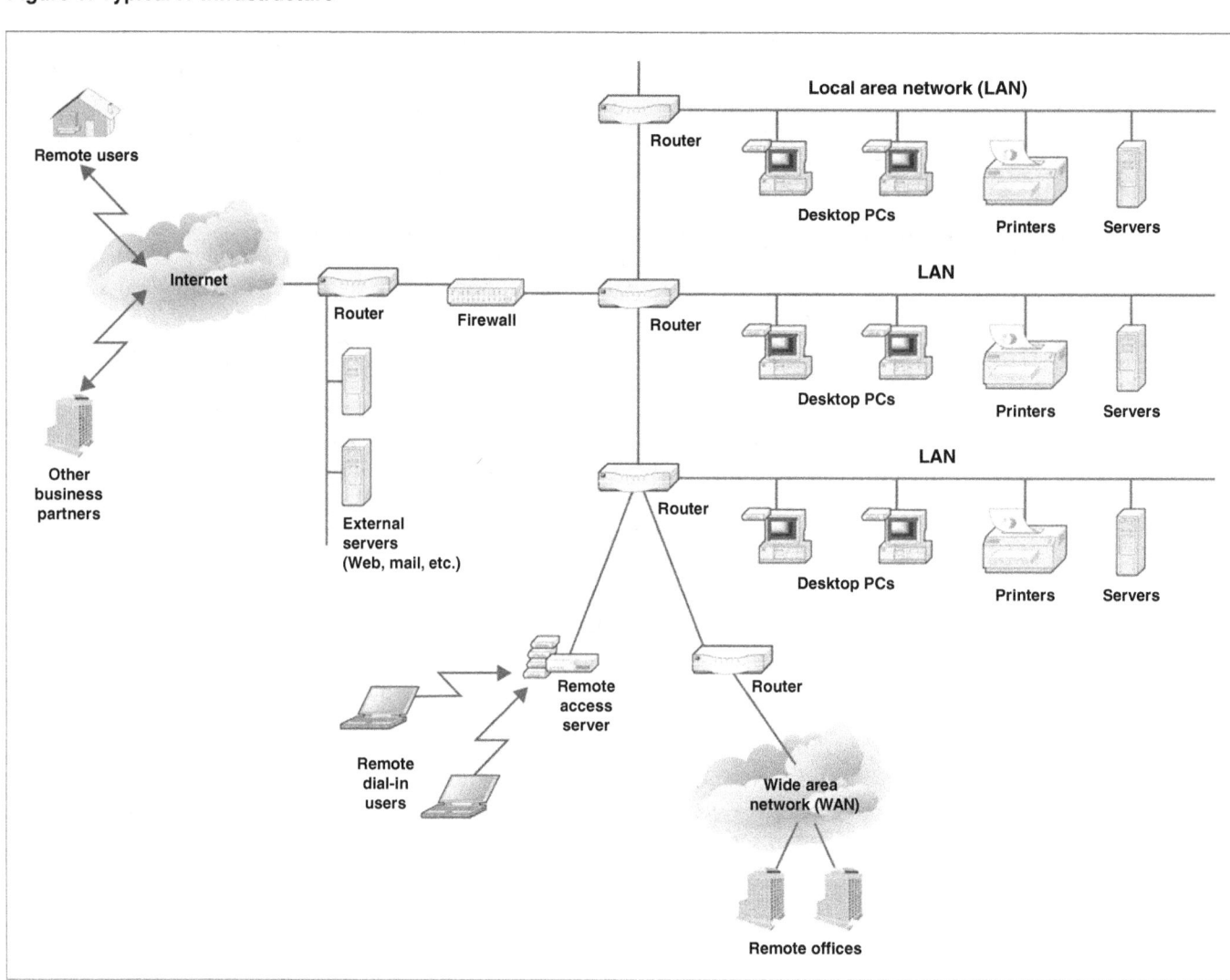

Source: GAO.

Commercially available cybersecurity technologies can be deployed to protect each of these components. These technologies implement the technical controls that NIST recommends federal agencies deploy in order to effectively meet federal requirements. They can be used to test effectiveness of the controls directly, monitor compliance with agency policies, and account for and analyze security incidents. In addition, current technologies can significantly assist an agency in reassessing previously identified risks, identifying new problem areas, reassessing the appropriateness of existing controls and security-related activities, identifying the need for new controls, and redirecting subsequent monitoring efforts.

Cybersecurity Technologies Can Be Categorized by Control Functionality

We enumerate cybersecurity technologies in a framework that is based on the five general categories of controls related to the security service or functionality that available technologies provide:

1. **Access controls** restrict the ability of unknown or unauthorized users to view or use information, hosts, or networks. Access control technologies can help protect sensitive data and systems.

2. **System integrity controls** are used to ensure that a system and its data are not illicitly modified or corrupted by malicious code.

3. **Cryptography controls** include encryption of data during transmission and when data are stored on a system. Encryption is the process of transforming ordinary data into code form so that the information is accessible only to those who are authorized to have access.

4. **Audit and monitoring controls** help administrators to perform investigations during and after an attack.

5. **Configuration management and assurance controls** help administrators to view and change the security settings on their hosts and networks, verify the correctness of security settings, and maintain operations in a secure fashion under duress conditions.

We frame our discussions of specific technologies around these categories. We introduce each general category and describe how the technologies work and their reported effectiveness. Table 2 lists the five control categories and a brief description of the technologies that support these categories.

Table 2: Cybersecurity Technology Control Categories and Technologies

	Technology	What it does
Access control		
Boundary protection	Firewalls	Control access to and from a network or computer.
	Content management	Monitors Web and messaging applications for inappropriate content, including spam, banned file types, and proprietary information.
Authentication	Biometrics	Uses human characteristics, such as fingerprints, irises, and voices, to establish the identity of the user.
	Smart tokens	Establish identity of users through an integrated circuit chip in a portable device, such as a smart card or a time-synchronized token.
Authorization	User rights and privileges	Allow or prevent access to data, systems, and actions of users based on the established policies of an organization.
System integrity	Antivirus software	Provides protection against malicious computer code, such as viruses, worms, and Trojan horses.
	Integrity checkers	Monitor alterations to files that are considered critical to an organization.
Cryptography	Digital signatures and certificates	Use public key cryptography to provide: (1) assurance that both the sender and the recipient of a message or transaction will be uniquely identified, (2) assurance that the data have not been accidentally or deliberately altered, and (3) verifiable proof of the integrity and origin of the data.
	Virtual private networks	Allow organizations or individuals in two or more physical locations to establish network connections over a shared or public network, such as the Internet, with functionality similar to that of a private network.
Audit and monitoring	Intrusion detection systems	Detect inappropriate, incorrect, or anomalous activity on a network or computer system.
	Intrusion prevention systems	Build on intrusion detection systems to detect attacks on a network and take action to prevent them from being successful.
	Security event correlation tools	Monitor and document actions on network devices and analyze the actions to determine if an attack is ongoing or has occurred. Enable an organization to determine if ongoing system activities are operating according to its security policy.
	Computer forensics tools	Identify, preserve, extract, and document computer-based evidence.
Configuration management and assurance	Policy enforcement applications	Enable system administrators to engage in centralized monitoring and enforcement of an organization's security policies.
	Network management	Allows for the control and monitoring of networks, including management of faults, configurations, performance, and security.
	Continuity of operations tools	Provide a complete backup infrastructure to maintain the availability of systems or networks in the event of an emergency or during planned maintenance.
	Scanners	Analyze computers or networks for security vulnerabilities.
	Patch management	Acquires, tests, and applies multiple patches to one or more computer systems.

Source: GAO analysis.

Access Controls

Access control technologies ensure that only authorized users or systems can access and use computers, networks, and the information stored on these systems, and these technologies help to protect sensitive data and systems. Access control simplifies network security by reducing the number of paths that attackers might use to penetrate system or network defenses. Access control includes three different control types: boundary protection, authentication, and authorization.

Boundary protection technologies demark a logical or physical boundary between protected information and systems and unknown users. Boundary protection technologies can be used to protect a network (for example, firewalls) or a single computer (for example, personal firewalls). Generally, these technologies prevent access to the network or computer by external unauthorized users. Another type of boundary protection technology, content management, can also be used to restrict the ability of authorized system or network users to access systems or networks beyond the system or network boundary.

Authentication technologies associate a user with a particular identity. People are authenticated by three basic means: by something they know, something they have, or something they are. People and systems regularly use these means to identify people in everyday life. For example, members of a community routinely recognize one another by how they look or how their voices sound—by something they are. Automated teller machines recognize customers because they present a bank card—something they have—and they enter a personal identification number (PIN)—something they know. Using a key to enter a locked building is another example of using something you have. More secure systems may combine two of more of these approaches.

While the use of passwords is an example of authentication based on something users know, there are several technologies based on something users have. Security tokens can be used to authenticate a user. User information can be coded onto a token using magnetic media (for example, bank cards) or optical media (for example, compact disk–like media). Several smart token technologies containing an integrated circuit chip that can store and process data are also available. Biometric technologies automate the identification of people using one or more of their distinct physical or behavioral characteristics—authentication based on something that users are. The use of security tokens or biometrics requires the installation of the appropriate readers at network and computer access points.

Once a user is authenticated, authorization technologies are used to allow or prevent actions by that user according to predefined rules. Users could be granted access to data on the system or to perform certain actions on the system. Authorization technologies support the principles of legitimate use, least privilege, and separation of duties. Access control could be based on user identity, role, group membership, or other information known to the system.

Most operating systems and some applications provide some authentication and authorization functionality. For example, user identification (ID) codes and passwords are the most commonly used authentication technology. System administrators can assign users rights and privileges to applications and data files based on user IDs. Some operating systems allow for the grouping of users to simplify the administration of groups of users who require the same levels of access to files and applications.

Boundary Protection: Firewalls

What the technology does

Firewalls are network devices or systems running special software that controls the flow of network traffic between networks or between a host and a network. A firewall is set up as the single point through which communications must pass. This enables the firewall to act as a protective barrier between the protected network and any external networks. Any information leaving the internal network can be forced to pass through a firewall as it leaves the network or host. Incoming data can enter only through the firewall.

Firewalls are typically deployed where a corporate network connects to the Internet. However, firewalls can also be used internally, to guard areas of an organization against unauthorized internal access. For example, many corporate networks use firewalls to restrict access to internal networks that perform sensitive functions, such as accounting or personnel.

Personal computers can also have firewalls, called personal firewalls, to protect them from unauthorized access over a network. Such personal firewalls are relatively inexpensive software programs that can be installed on personal computers to filter all network traffic and allow only authorized communications. Essentially, a firewall can be likened to a protective fence that keeps unwanted external data out and sensitive internal data in (see fig. 2).

Figure 2: A Typical Firewall Protecting Hosts on a Private Network from the Public Network

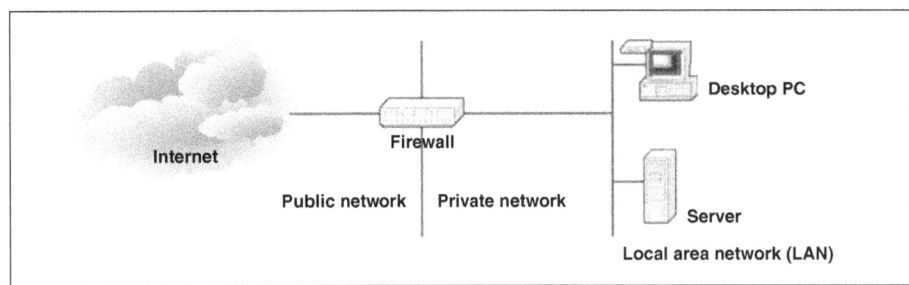

Source: GAO analysis.

How the technology works

Typically, a firewall is a network device or host with two or more network interfaces—one connected to the protected internal network and the other connected to unprotected networks, such as the Internet. The firewall runs software that examines the network packets arriving at its network interfaces and takes appropriate action based on a set of rules. The idea is to define these rules so that they allow only authorized network traffic to flow between the two interfaces. Configuring the firewall involves setting up the rules properly. One configuration strategy is to reject all network traffic and then enable only a limited set of network packets to go through the firewall. The authorized network traffic would include the connections necessary to perform functions like visiting Web sites and receiving electronic mail.

NIST describes eight kinds of firewalls: packet filter firewalls, stateful inspection firewalls, application proxy gateway firewalls, dedicated proxy firewalls, hybrid firewall technologies, network address translation, host-based firewalls, and personal firewalls/personal firewall appliances.[17]

Packet filter firewalls are routing devices that include access control functionality for system addresses and communication sessions. The

---

[17]National Institute of Standards and Technology, *Guidelines for Firewalls and Firewall Policy*, NIST Special Publication 800-41, (January 2002).

access control functionality of a packet filter firewall is governed by a set of rules that allows or blocks network packets based on a number of their characteristics, including the source and destination addresses, the network protocol, and the source and destination port numbers. Packet filter firewalls are usually placed at the outermost boundary with an untrusted network, and they form the first line of defense. An example of a packet filter firewall is a network router that employs filter rules to screen network traffic.

Stateful inspection firewalls keep track of network connections that are used by network applications to reliably transfer data. When an application uses a network connection to create a session with a remote host system, a port is also opened on the originating system. This port receives network traffic from the destination system. For successful connections, packet filter firewalls must permit inbound packets from the destination system. Opening up many ports to incoming traffic creates a risk of intrusion by unauthorized users, who may employ a variety of techniques to abuse the expected conventions of network protocols such as Transmission Control Protocol (TCP). Stateful inspection firewalls solve this problem by creating a directory of outbound network connections, along with each session's corresponding client port. This "state table" is then used to validate any inbound traffic. The stateful inspection solution is more secure than a packet filter because it tracks client ports individually rather than opening all inbound ports for external access.

Application proxy gateway firewalls provide additional protection by inserting the firewall as an intermediary between internal applications that attempt to communicate with external servers such as a Web server. For example, a Web proxy receives requests for external Web pages from inside the firewall and relays them to the exterior Web server as though the firewall were the requesting Web client. The external Web server responds to the firewall and the firewall forwards the response to the inside client as though the firewall were the Web server. No direct network connection is ever made from the inside client host to the external Web server.

Dedicated proxy servers are typically deployed behind traditional firewall platforms. In typical use, a main firewall might accept inbound network traffic, determine which application is being targeted, and then hand off the traffic to the appropriate proxy server (for example, an e-mail proxy server). The proxy server typically would perform filtering or logging operations on the traffic and then forward it to internal systems. A proxy server could also accept outbound traffic directly from internal systems, filter or log the traffic, and then pass it to the firewall for outbound delivery. Many organizations enable the caching of frequently used Web pages on the proxy server, thereby reducing firewall traffic. In addition to possessing authentication and logging functionality, dedicated proxy servers are useful for Web and electronic mail content scanning.

Hybrid firewall technologies are firewall products that incorporate functionality from several different types of firewall platforms. For example, many vendors of packet filter firewalls or stateful inspection packet filter firewalls have implemented basic application proxy functionality to offset some of the weaknesses associated with their firewall platforms. In most cases, these vendors implement application proxies to provide improved logging of network traffic and stronger user authentication. Nearly all major firewall vendors have introduced multiple firewall functions into their products in some manner; therefore it is not always a simple matter to decide which specific firewall product is the most suitable for a given application or enterprise infrastructure. Selection of a hybrid firewall product should be based on the supported feature sets that an enterprise needs.

Network address translation (NAT) technology is an effective tool for "hiding" the network addresses of an internal network behind a firewall environment. In essence, NAT allows an organization to deploy a network addressing plan of its choosing behind a firewall while still maintaining the ability to connect to external systems through the firewall. Network address translation is accomplished by one of three methods: static, hiding, and port. In static NAT, each internal system on the private network has a corresponding external, routable Internet protocol (IP) address associated with it. This particular technique is seldom used because unique IP addresses are in short supply. With hiding NAT, all systems behind a firewall share the same external, routable IP address, while the internal systems use private IP addresses. Thus, with a hiding NAT system, a number of systems behind a firewall will appear to be a single system. With port address translation, it is possible to place hosts behind a firewall system and still make them selectively accessible to external users.

Host-based firewalls are firewall software components that are available in some operating systems or as add-ons. Because a network-based firewall cannot fully protect internal servers, host-based firewalls can be used to secure individual hosts.

Personal firewalls and personal firewall appliances are used to secure PCs at home or remote locations. These firewalls are important because many personnel telecommute or work at home and access sensitive data. Home users dialing an ISP may potentially have limited firewall protection available to them because the ISP has to accommodate many different security policies. Therefore, personal firewalls have been developed to provide protection for remote systems and to perform many of the same functions as larger firewalls. These products are typically implemented in one of two configurations. The first configuration is a personal firewall, which is installed on the system it is meant to protect; personal firewalls usually do not offer protection to other systems or resources. Likewise, personal firewalls do not typically provide controls over network traffic that is traversing a computer network—they protect only the computer system on which they are installed. The second configuration is a personal firewall appliance. In most cases, personal firewall appliances are designed to protect small networks such as networks that might be found in home offices. These appliances usually run on specialized hardware and integrate some other form of network infrastructure components into the firewall itself, including the following: cable or digital subscriber line broadband modem with network routing, network hub, network switch, dynamic host configuration protocol (DHCP) server, simple network management protocol (SNMP) agent, and application proxy agents. In terms of deployment strategies, personal firewalls and personal firewall appliances normally address connectivity concerns that are associated with telecommuters or branch offices. However, some organizations employ these devices on their organizational intranets, practicing a layered defense strategy.

Centrally managed distributed firewalls are centrally controlled but locally enforced. A security administrator—not the end users—defines and maintains security policies. This places the responsibility and capability of defining security policies in the hands of a security professional who can properly lock down the target systems. A centrally managed system is scalable because it is unnecessary to administer each system separately. A properly executed distributed firewall system includes exception logging. More advanced systems include the capability to enforce the appropriate policy, which is enforced depending on the location of the firewall. Centrally managed distributed firewalls can be either software- or hardware-based firewalls. Centrally managed distributed software firewalls are similar in function and features to host-based or personal firewalls, but their security policies are centrally defined and managed. Centrally managed distributed hardware firewalls combine the filtering capability of a firewall with the connectivity capability of a traditional connection.

Effectiveness of the technology

When properly configured, all firewalls can protect a network or a PC from unauthorized access through the network. Although firewalls afford protection of certain resources within an organization, there are some threats that firewalls cannot protect against: connections that bypass the firewall, new threats that have not yet been identified, and viruses that have been injected into the internal network. It is important to consider these shortcomings in addition to the firewall itself in order to counter these additional threats and provide a comprehensive security solution. Each type of firewall platform has its own strengths and weaknesses.

Packet filter firewalls have two main strengths: speed and flexibility. Packet filter firewalls can be used to secure nearly any type of network communication or protocol. This versatility allows packet filter firewalls to be deployed into nearly any enterprise network infrastructure. Packet filter firewalls have several weaknesses: They cannot prevent attacks that exploit application-specific vulnerabilities or functions; they can log only a minimal amount of information—such as source address, destination address, and traffic type; they do not support user authentication; and they are vulnerable to attacks and exploits that take advantage of flaws within the TCP/IP protocol, such as IP address spoofing.[18]

Stateful inspection firewalls share the strengths and weaknesses of packet filter firewalls, but because of the state table implementation, they are generally considered to be more secure than packet filter firewalls. Stateful inspection firewalls can accommodate other network protocols in the same manner that packet filters do, but stateful inspection technology is relevant only to the TCP/IP protocol.

Application proxy gateway firewalls have numerous advantages over packet filter firewalls and stateful inspection firewalls. First, application proxy gateway firewalls are able to examine the entire network packet rather than only the network addresses and ports. This enables these firewalls to provide more extensive logging capabilities than packet filters

---

[18]IP address spoofing involves altering the address information in network packets in order to make packets appear to come from a trusted IP address.

or stateful inspection firewalls do. Another advantage is that application proxy gateway firewalls can authenticate users directly, while packet filter firewalls and stateful inspection firewalls normally authenticate users based on the network address of their system (i.e., source, destination, and type). Given that network addresses can be easily spoofed, the authentication capabilities inherent in application proxy gateway architecture are superior to those found in packet filter or stateful inspection firewalls. The advanced functionality of application proxy gateway firewalls also results in several disadvantages when compared with the functionality of packet filter or stateful inspection firewalls. First, because of the "full packet awareness" found in application proxy gateways, the firewall is forced to spend significant time reading and interpreting each packet. Therefore, application proxy gateway firewalls are generally not well suited to high-bandwidth or real-time applications. To reduce the load on the firewall, a dedicated proxy server can be used to secure less time-sensitive services, such as e-mail and most Web traffic. Another disadvantage is that application proxy gateway firewalls are often limited in terms of support for new network applications and protocols. An individual, application-specific proxy agent is required for each type of network traffic that needs to go through the firewall. Most vendors of application proxy gateways provide generic proxy agents to support undefined network protocols or applications. However, those generic agents tend to negate many of the strengths of the application proxy gateway architecture, and they simply allow traffic to "tunnel" through the firewall.

Dedicated proxy servers allow an organization to enforce user authentication requirements and other filtering and logging of any traffic that goes through the proxy server. This means that an organization can restrict outbound traffic to certain locations, examine all outbound e-mail for viruses, or restrict internal users from writing to the organization's Web server. Because most security problems originate from within an organization, proxy servers can assist in foiling internally based attacks or malicious behavior.

In terms of strengths and weaknesses, each type of NAT—static, hiding, or port—is applicable in certain situations; the variable is the amount of design flexibility offered by each type. Static NAT offers the most flexibility, but it is not always practical because of the shortage of IP addresses. Hiding NAT technology it is seldom used because port address translation offers additional features. Port address translation is often the most convenient and secure solution.

Host-based firewall packages typically provide access control capability for restricting traffic to and from servers that run on the host, and logging is usually available. A disadvantage of host-based firewalls is that they must be administered separately, and maintaining security becomes more difficult as the number of configured devices increases.

Centrally managed distributed software firewalls have the benefit of unified corporate oversight of firewall implementation on individual machines. However, they remain vulnerable to attacks on the host operating system from the networks, as well as to intentional or unintentional tampering by users logging in to the system that is being protected. Centrally managed distributed hardware firewalls filter the data on the firewall hardware rather on than the host system. This can make the distributed hardware firewall system less vulnerable than software-based distributed firewalls. Hardware distributed firewalls can be designed to be unaffected by local or network attacks via the host operating systems. Performance and throughput of a hardware firewall system are generally better than they are for software systems.

Boundary Protection: Content Management

What the technology does

Content filters monitor Web and messaging applications for inappropriate content, spam, intellectual property breach, noncompliance with an organization's security policies, and banned file types.[19] The filters can help to keep illegal material out of an organization's systems, reduce network traffic from spam, and stop various types of cyber attacks. They can also keep track of which users are browsing the Web, when, where, and for how long.

There are three main types of content filters: (1) Web filters, which screen and exclude from access or availability Web pages that are deemed objectionable or non–business related; (2) messaging filters, which screen messaging applications such as e-mail, instant messaging, short message service, and peer-to-peer for spam or other objectionable content; and

---

[19]Spam is electronic junk mail that is unsolicited and usually is advertising for some product. An intellectual property breach can include client information, trade secrets, ongoing research, and other such information that has not been authorized for release.

(3) Web integrity filters, which ensure the integrity of an entity's Web pages. [20]

How the technology works

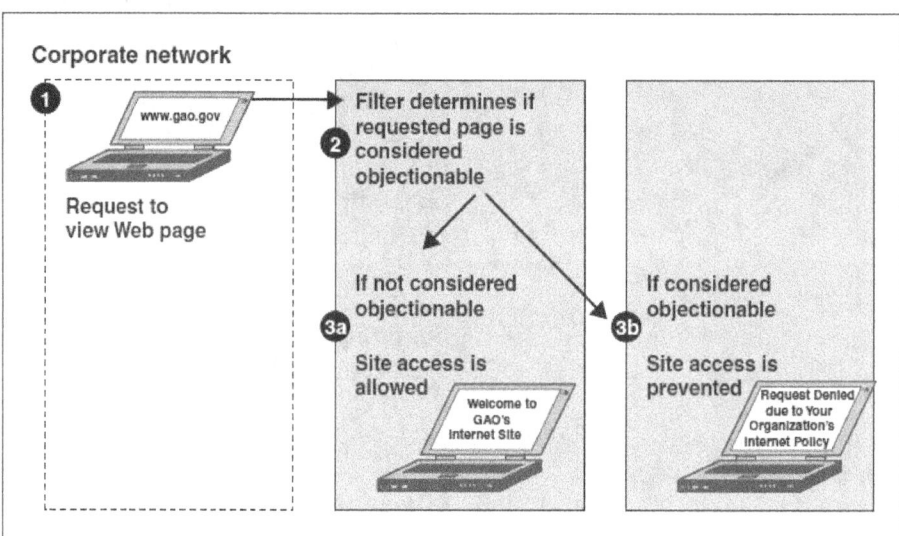

Source: GAO analysis.

Web filters screen and block objectionable Web pages by (1) intercepting a user's request to view a Web page, (2) determining that the requested page contains objectionable content, and (3) prohibiting the user from accessing that Web page (see fig. 3). Web filters can observe and respond to requests in two main ways. One method, pass-through technology, requires the Web filtration software to be integrated with other network devices such as proxies or gateways. This ensures that all requests pass through the Web filter to be accepted or denied. Another method of handling requests, known as pass-by technology, requires that the Web filtration software be installed on a stand-alone server and placed on the

---

[20]Short message service is the transmission of short text messages to and from a mobile phone, a fax machine, or an IP address. Messages must be no longer than 160 alphanumeric characters and contain no images or graphics. On the Internet, peer-to-peer (referred to as P2P) networks allow computer users to share files from one another's hard drives. Napster, Gnutella, and Kazaa are examples of peer-to-peer software.

GAO-04-467 Information Security

network of machines that it is to filter. The Web filter then receives all of the traffic that exists on the network, but it does not prevent the network traffic from reaching its intended destination. If a request is made for a restricted Web page, the Web filter will display an error message stating that the user's access to the Web page has been denied. The user's connection with the Web site is then closed to prevent the Web server from sending additional information to the user's computer. Web filters also vary in their methods of determining if a requested Web page contains objectionable material:

- **Site classification** technology compares the requested Web site against a database of Web pages that are considered objectionable. Typically, vendors provide a basic database of objectionable Web pages as part of the Web filter software, which may then be modified by an administrator. Vendors often provide subscription services so customers' databases can be automatically updated with new sites that have been found to be objectionable. The database consists primarily of a list of Web site addresses, typically categorized in groups such as gambling, adult material, and sports. An administrator can then decide which sites should be blocked, based on the category they fall into. If the requested Web site is on the list of objectionable Web sites, the Web filter will display a message informing the user that he or she has been denied access to the Web page.

- **Content classification** uses artificial intelligence in conjunction with site classification techniques to maintain an updated database. Before a user can view a Web site, the Web filter examines the textual content of the Web page, the source code, and metatags.[21] Questionable content is identified by the presence of key words or phrases or by a combination of key word frequency and level of obscenity of the words. Web sites found to be objectionable based on their content can then be added to the database of objectionable sites, and the user would not be allowed to view them. Web sites do not have to be blocked for an entire organization, but can be blocked based on IP address ranges, host names, or other criteria.

Messaging filters operate similarly to Web filters and can examine the content of a message to filter out spam, offensive language, or recreational e-mails that lower the productivity of workers. Messaging filters also block

---

[21]The source code is the text of a program while it is still in its programming language. The Hypertext Markup Language (HTML) metatag is used to describe the contents of a Web page.

messages based on the types of file attachments and the senders of the e-mails, as determined by an organization's policy. Files are excluded based on their file extensions, or the last part of their name, which indicates the file type. The files might be excluded to limit the trafficking of illicit material, stop viruses from entering the network, limit intellectual property breaches, or carry out other such functions intended to increase the security of an organization. File extensions that are typically excluded are MP3 (music files), JPG (graphic files), MPEG (video files), and EXE (executable files), among others.

A Web integrity filter ensures the integrity of the content of a Web page. If a Web server is attacked or becomes inaccessible to users, the Web integrity filter attempts to keep unauthorized information from being released to the public, and only the original content would still go out. The content filter is a separate device on the network, located between the Web server and the router or firewall. The device contains a collection of digital signatures of authorized Web content that is known to be legitimate. When a request is made to the Web server, each object's digital signature is compared with the digital signature that the device had previously collected.[22] If the digital signatures do not match, the page is considered to be unauthorized and it is immediately replaced with a secure archived copy of the original page, and the software notifies the appropriate personnel via phone, e-mail, or pager.

Effectiveness of the technology

Content filters have significant rates of both erroneously accepting objectionable sites and blocking sites that are not objectionable. If implemented correctly, filtering can reduce the volume of unsolicited and undesired e-mails. However, it is not completely accurate, and legitimate messages might get blocked. Also, some content filters do not work with all operating systems.

While pass-through technology can be effective at stopping specified traffic, there are several disadvantages to using it. First, because the requests for Web sites are actually stopped at the gateway while the filtering product analyzes the request against its rules, a certain amount of

---

[22]An object can be an HTML page, a graphics file, a music file, and so forth.

latency can result, especially during periods of high traffic volume.[23] Second, pass-through products might be considered a single point of failure: If the product fails, so might Internet connectivity. Third, because pass-through devices are dependent on another network device, if an entity changes firewalls or proxy servers, it might have to purchase a new content filter product as well. Pass-by technology can also be effective at stopping specified traffic. Because traffic does not have to be screened before it goes through, the pass-by technology does not cause latency. Also, because pass-by products do not require integration with other network devices, a change in a firewall or proxy would not result in a need to change the content filtering product. However, a disadvantage of the pass-by solution is that a separate server must be dedicated to performing the monitoring and filtering functions.

Site classification is effective in keeping users from accessing sites that have been determined to have objectionable content. However, because of the size and growth of the Internet, this technology faces challenges in keeping full and accurate lists of objectionable sites, and the cost of subscriptions for updates can be very expensive. Content classification can assist in classifying new sites without the cost of subscribing to an update service, but this method has its drawbacks as well. First, Web sites that are predominantly graphical in nature may not contain enough key words for the program to categorize the site. Second, there are some topics that are so ambiguous that it is very difficult to classify them by their content. Third, users may circumvent the filtered lists by using proxy sites.

Authentication: Biometrics

What the technology does

The term *biometrics* covers a wide range of technologies that are used to verify identity by measuring and analyzing human characteristics. Biometric technologies are authentication techniques that rely on measuring and analyzing physiological or behavioral characteristics. Identifying an individual's physiological characteristic involves measuring a part of the body, such as fingertips or eye irises; identifying behavioral characteristics involves deriving data from actions, such as speech.

---

[23]Latency is the amount of time it takes a packet to travel from source to destination. Together, latency and bandwidth define the speed and capacity of a network.

Biometrics are theoretically very effective personal identifiers because the characteristics they measure are thought to be distinct to each person. Unlike conventional identification methods that use something you have (for example, a smart card), or something you know (for example, a password), these characteristics are integral to something you are. Because they are tightly bound to an individual, they are more reliable, cannot be forgotten, and are less easily lost, stolen, or guessed.

How the technology works

Although biometric technologies vary in complexity, capabilities, and performance, they all share several elements. Biometric identification systems are essentially pattern recognition systems. They use acquisition devices such as cameras and scanning devices to capture images, recordings, or measurements of an individual's characteristics, and they use computer hardware and software to extract, encode, store, and compare these characteristics. Because the process is automated, biometric decision making is generally very fast, in most cases taking only a few seconds in real time. The different types of biometric technologies measure different characteristics. However, they all involve a similar process, which can be divided into two distinct stages: (1) enrollment and (2) verification or identification.

Enrollment stage. Acquisition devices such as cameras and scanners are used to capture images, recordings, or measurements of an individual's characteristics, and computer hardware and software are used to extract, encode, store, and compare these characteristics. In the enrollment stage, the captured samples are averaged and processed to generate a unique digital representation of the characteristic, called a reference template, which is stored for future comparisons. It is impossible to recreate the sample, such as a fingerprint, from the template. Templates can be stored centrally on a computer database, within the device itself, or on a smart card.

Verification or identification stage. Depending on the application, biometric technologies can be used in one of two modes: verification or identification. Verification is used to verify a person's identity, answering the question "Is this person who she claims to be?" Identification is used to establish a person's identity, comparing the individual's biometric with all stored biometric records to answer the question "Who is this person?"

Current biometric technologies that are used to protect computer systems from unauthorized access include fingerprint recognition, iris recognition, and speaker recognition. These technologies are used by some entities to replace passwords as a way to authenticate individuals who are attempting to access computers and networks

Fingerprint recognition technology extracts features from impressions that are made by the distinctive ridges on the fingertips. An image of the fingerprint is captured by a scanner, enhanced, and converted into a template. Various styles of fingerprint scanners are commercially available. The scanner can be built into the computer or into the mouse or the keyboard that is attached to the computer, or it can be a hardware device that is used exclusively for capturing fingerprints (see figs. 4 and 5).

Figure 4: An Example of Fingerprint Recognition Technology Built into a Keyboard

Source: Key Tronic Corporation.

Figure 5: An Example of Fingerprint Recognition Technology Built into a Mouse

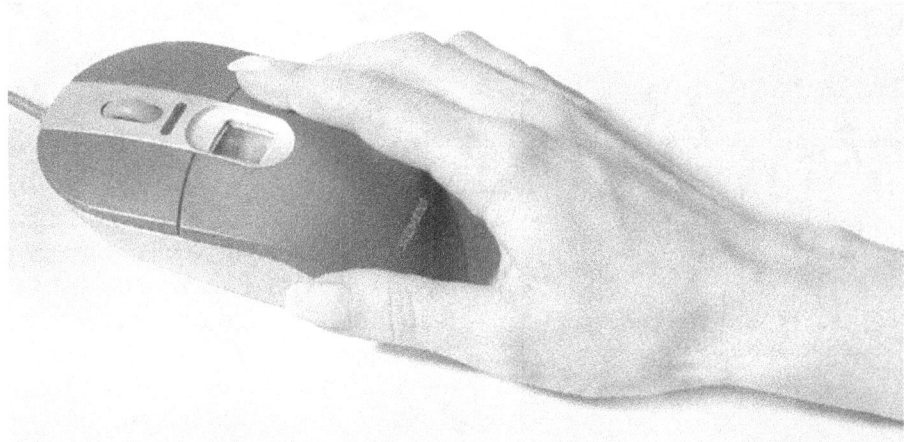

Source: Siemens PSE TechLab.

Iris recognition technology is based on the distinctly colored ring surrounding the pupil of the eye. Made from elastic connective tissue, the iris is a very rich source of biometric data, having approximately 266

distinct characteristics. Iris recognition systems use a small, high-quality camera to capture a black-and-white, high-resolution image of the iris. The boundaries of the iris are defined and a coordinate system is established over the iris before visible characteristics are converted into a template (see fig. 6).

Figure 6: A Desktop Iris Recognition System

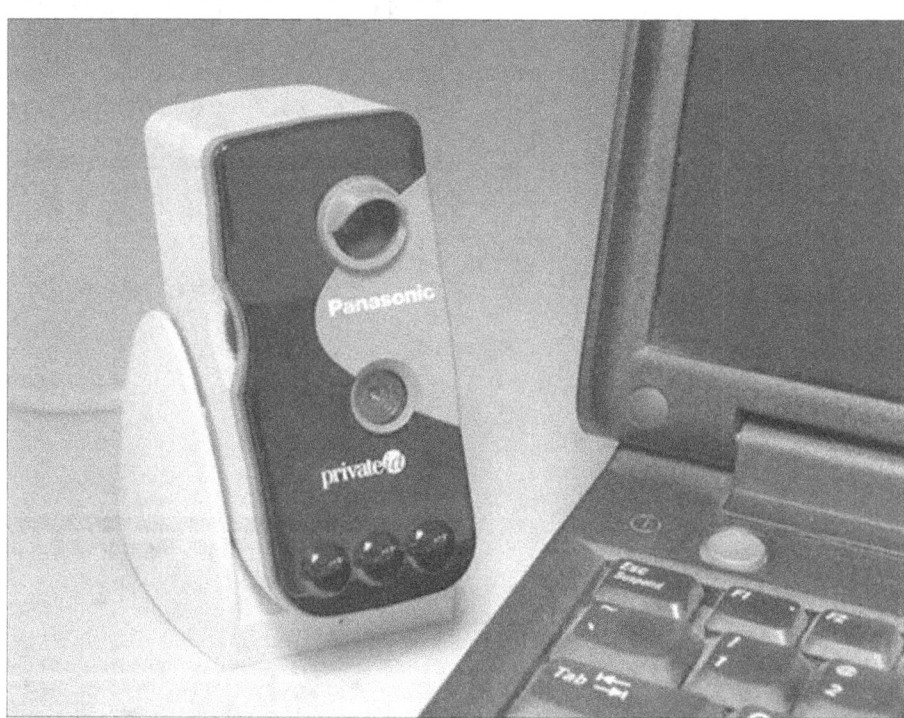

Source: Matsushita Electric Corporation of America.

Speaker recognition technology uses the distinctive characteristics in the sound of people's voices as a biometric identifier. These characteristics result from a combination of physiological differences in the shape of vocal tracts and learned speaking habits. Speaker recognition systems capture samples of a person's speech by having him or her speak into a microphone or telephone a number of times. Some systems require that a predefined phrase, such as a name or a sequence of numbers, be used for enrollment. This phrase is converted from analog to digital format, and the distinctive vocal characteristics, such as pitch, cadence, and tone, are extracted to create a template.

Effectiveness of the technology

The quality of the templates is critical in the overall success of a biometric system. Minute changes in positioning, distance, pressure, environment, and other factors influence the generation of a template. For example, in a speaker recognition system, performance can be affected by background noise, the use of different capture devices for enrollment and verification, speaking softly, and poor placement of the capture device. In addition, because biometric features can change over time, people may have to re-enroll to update their reference templates.

Furthermore, not all people can use biometric technologies. For example, the capturing of fingerprints for about 2 to 5 percent of people is not possible because the fingerprints are dirty or have become dry or worn from age, extensive manual labor, or exposure to corrosive chemicals. People who are mute cannot use speaker recognition systems, and people lacking fingers or eyes from congenital disease, surgery, or injury cannot use fingerprint or iris recognition systems.

The effectiveness of biometric technologies is affected by the quality of the capture device. For example, some fingerprint recognition scanners can be prone to error if there is a buildup of dirt, grime, or oil—producing leftover fingerprints from previous users, known as latent prints. Severe latent prints can cause the superimposition of two sets of prints and degrade the capturing of the image. Similarly, the performance of speaker recognition systems improves with higher-quality input devices.

Tests have shown that certain capture devices can be tricked into accepting forgeries. Fingerprint scanners have been tricked into accepting latent prints that were reactivated simply by breathing on the sensor or by placing a water-filled plastic bag on the sensor's surface. It is possible to reconstruct and authenticate latent fingerprints by dusting the sensor's surface with commercially available graphite powder and lifting the fingerprint with adhesive tape. A vulnerability of speaker authentication is that the voice can be easily recorded and therefore duplicated. However, some speaker verification systems provide safeguards against the use of a recorded voice to trick the system. For these systems, the electronic properties of a recording device, particularly the playback speaker, will change the acoustics to such a degree that the recorded voice sample will not match a stored voiceprint of a live voice.

What the technology does

A smart token is an easily portable device that contains an embedded integrated circuit chip that is capable of both storing and processing data. Most smart tokens are used instead of static user IDs and passwords to provide a stronger and more convenient means for users to identify and authenticate themselves to computers and networks. When it is used for this function, a smart token is an example of authentication based on something a user possesses (in this case, the token itself). Although authentication for some computer systems is based solely on the possession of a token, typical smart token implementations also require a user to provide something he or she knows (for example, a password) in order to successfully utilize the smart token.[24]

How the technology works

In general, smart tokens can be classified according to physical characteristics, interfaces, and protocols used. These classifications are not mutually exclusive.

1. **Physical characteristics**. Smart tokens can be divided into two physical groups: smart cards and other tokens. A smart card looks like a credit card but includes an embedded microprocessor. Smart tokens that are not smart cards can look like calculators, keys, or other small objects.

2. **Interfaces**. Smart tokens have either a human or an electronic interface. Smart tokens that look like calculators usually have a human interface, which allows humans to communicate with the device. Other smart tokens, including smart cards, have an electronic interface that can only be understood by special readers and writers. Two physical interfaces for smart cards have been standardized through the International Organization for Standardization, resulting in two types of smart cards. The first type, known as contact cards, works by inserting the card in a smart card reader, while the second type, known as contactless cards, uses radio frequency signals, and the card needs

---

[24]See U.S. General Accounting Office, *Electronic Government: Progress in Promoting Adoption of Smart Card Technology,* GAO-03-144 (Washington, D.C.: January 3, 2003) for our report on the use of smart cards in the federal government.

only to be passed within proximity to a card terminal to transmit information. Smart cards can be configured to include both contact and contactless capabilities, but because standards for the two technologies are very different, two separate interfaces would be needed.

3. **Protocols**. Smart tokens use three main methods for authentication, based on different protocols. The first method, static password exchange, requires users to first authenticate themselves to a token before the token can then authenticate the user to the computer. The other two methods are known as time-synchronized and challenge-response, and are based on cryptography. These methods generate a onetime password, which is a password or pass code that can be used only once, for a brief interval, and then is no longer valid. If it is intercepted in any way, the password has such a limited life span that it quickly becomes invalid. The next time the same user attempts to access a system, he or she must enter a new onetime password that is generated by the security token.

Time-synchronized tokens generate a unique value that changes at regular intervals (e.g., once a minute). A central server keeps track of the token-generated passwords in order to compare the input against the expected value. To log onto a system, users enter a onetime password that consists of their personal PIN followed by the unique value generated by their token. The PIN helps the central server to identify the user and the password value that should be entered. If the number entered by the user and the one generated by the server are the same, the user will be granted access to the system. Figure 7 shows an example of a time-synchronized token.

Figure 7: Example of a Time-Synchronized Token

Source: RSA Security Inc.

Challenge-response tokens utilize a central server to generate a challenge (such as a random string of numbers), which a user would then enter into the token. The token then calculates a response that serves as a onetime numeric password that is entered into the system. If the response from the user is the same as the response expected by the server, the user will be granted access to the system. In some implementations, the user must enter a PIN before the server will generate a challenge. Figure 8 is an example of a challenge-response token.

Figure 8: Example of a Challenge-Response Token

Source: © 2004 Secure Computing Corporation.

Effectiveness of the technology

If they are implemented correctly, smart tokens can help to create a secure authentication environment. Onetime passwords eliminate the problem of electronic monitoring, or "password sniffing," and tokens that require the use of a PIN help to reduce the risk of forgery.

However, smart tokens do not necessarily verify a person's identity; they only confirm that a person has the token. Because tokens can be lost or stolen, an attacker could obtain a token and attempt to determine the user's PIN number or password. If an older algorithm is used to formulate a onetime password, it is possible that modern computers could crack the algorithm used to formulate the random numbers that are generated by a token. For these reasons, these technologies are generally not considered acceptable as stand-alone systems to protect extremely sensitive data, and additional controls—such as biometric identification—may be required. As a result, smart token systems are considered more effective when combined with other methods of authentication.

In addition, at times the token could become unavailable to the user. For example, tokens can be broken, their batteries eventually discharge, and users could simply forget to bring tokens to work. For these reasons, organizations need to have an effective policy on how legitimate users can access systems without a token. If the policy is weak or poorly implemented, the security of the authentication system is weakened.

A problem that can arise with time-synchronized tokens is that the token and the central authentication server can get out of sync. If the token's clock drifts significantly ahead of or behind the server's clock, the authentication server may be vulnerable to a cryptographic attack.

Authorization: User Rights and Privileges

What the technology does

User rights and privileges grant or deny access to a protected resource, whether it is a network, a system, an individual computer, a program, or a file. These technologies authorize appropriate actions for users and prevent unauthorized access to data and systems. Typically, user rights and privileges are capabilities that are built into an operating system. For example, most operating systems include the concept of read, write, or read-and-write privileges for files and the capability to assign these privileges to users or groups of users.

Mainframe-based access control software controls users' entry to the system, their access to data on the system, and the level of usage available to them with program and other logical resources on the system.

Administrators can use these software tools to perform many access control functions—including identifying system users and authorizing user access to protected resources—while also ensuring individual accountability and logging unauthorized attempts at gaining access to the system and protected resources.

Additionally, some communication protocols can be used to control dial-up access into networks. Protocols that provide these services include Terminal Access Controller Access System (TACACS+), which centrally manages multiple connections to a single user, a network or subnetwork and interconnected networks, and Remote Authentication Dial-In User Service (RADIUS), which provides central authentication, authorization, and logging.

How the technology works

Mainframe-based access control software uses algorithms to determine whether to grant a user access to specific files, programs, or other defined resources (such as a printer queue or disk space to run a program). These algorithms are typically customized by a security administrator and result in access rules that are either user- or resource-based. User-based rules can be created to specify access for individuals or for groups. When access is requested, the software first identifies and authenticates the user, then it determines what resource that the user is requesting access to, and then it refers to the access rules before permitting the user to gain access to protected system resources. Access is denied to unauthorized users, and any authorized or unauthorized attempt to gain access can be logged.

Technologies that use resource-based rules assign a security classification to both users and data files in the form of security levels and categories. The levels and categories of a user and a resource are compared to determine whether the user has sufficient privileges to access a file or other resource.

The TACACS+ protocol allows a separate access server to independently provide the services of authentication, authorization, and accounting: The authentication service allows a user to use the same user name and password for multiple servers, which may employ different communication protocols. TACACS+ forwards the user's user name and password information to a centralized database that also has the TACACS+ protocol. This database then compares the log-in information to determine whether to grant or deny access to the user.

RADIUS is implemented in a client/server network architecture, where a centralized server using the RADIUS protocol maintains a database of all user authentication and network service access information for several client computers that also use the protocol. When a user logs on to the network via a RADIUS client, the user's password is encrypted and sent to the RADIUS server along with the user name. If the user name and password are correct, the server sends an acknowledgment message that includes information on the user's network system and service requirements. If the log-in process conditions are met, the user is authenticated and is given access to the requested network services.

Effectiveness of the technology

An operating system's built-in user rights and privileges can be effective when they are used with a well-defined security policy that guides who can access which resources.

A key component in implementing adequate access controls is ensuring that appropriate user rights and privileges have been assigned. If any one user has too many rights or has rights to a few key functions, the organization can be susceptible to fraud. Limiting user rights and privileges ensures that users have only the access they need to perform their duties, that very sensitive resources are limited to a few individuals, and that employees are restricted from performing incompatible functions or functions that are beyond their responsibilities. Excluding both roles and user rights reduces the possibility of fraudulent acts against the organization.

System Integrity

System integrity technologies are used to ensure that a system and its data are not illicitly modified or corrupted by malicious code. Malicious code includes viruses, Trojan horses, and worms. A virus is a program that infects computer files, usually executable programs, by inserting a copy of itself into the file. These copies are usually executed when a user takes some action, such as opening an infected e-mail attachment or executing a downloaded file that includes the virus. When executed, the virus can infect other files. Unlike a computer worm, a virus requires human involvement (usually unwitting) to propagate. A Trojan horse is a computer program that conceals harmful code. A Trojan horse usually masquerades as a useful program that a user would wish to execute. A worm is an independent computer program that reproduces by copying itself from one system to another. Unlike a computer virus, a worm does not require human involvement to propagate.

Antivirus software and integrity checkers are two types of technologies that help to protect against malicious code attacks. Antivirus software can be installed on computers to detect either incoming malicious code or malicious code that is already resident on the system—and to repair files that have been damaged by the code. Integrity checkers are usually applied to critical files or groups of files on a computer system. These programs typically take a snapshot of the files of interest and periodically compare the files with the snapshot to ensure that no unauthorized changes have been made.

Antivirus Software

What the technology does

Antivirus software provides protection against viruses and malicious code, such as worms and Trojan horses, by detecting and removing the malicious code and by preventing unwanted effects and repairing damage that may have resulted. Antivirus software uses a variety of techniques—such as signature scanners, activity blockers, and heuristic scanners—to protect computer systems against potentially harmful viruses, worms, and Trojan horses.

How the technology works

Antivirus software products can use a combination of the following technologies:

Signature scanners can identify known malicious code. Scanners search for "signature strings" or use algorithmic detection methods to identify known code. They rely on a significant amount of prior knowledge about the malicious code. Therefore, it is critical that the signature information for scanners be current. Most scanners can be configured to automatically update their signature information from a designated source, typically on a weekly basis; scanners can also be forced to update their signatures on demand.

Activity (or behavior) blockers contain a list of rules that a legitimate program must follow. If the program breaks one of the rules, the activity blockers alert the users. The idea is that untrusted code is first checked for improper behavior. If none is found, the code can be run in a restricted environment, where dynamic checks are performed on each potentially dangerous action before it is permitted to take effect. By adding multiple layers of reviews and checks to the execution process, activity blockers can prevent malicious code from performing undesirable actions.

Heuristic scanners work to protect against known viruses and are also able to detect unknown viruses. Heuristic scanners can be classified as either static or dynamic. Static heuristic scanners use virus signatures, much like standard signature scanners, but instead of scanning for specific viruses, they scan for lines of code that are associated with viruslike behaviors. These scanners are often supplemented by additional programs that search for more complex, viruslike behavior patterns. Dynamic heuristic scanners identify suspicious files and load them into a simulated computer system to emulate their execution. This allows the scanner to determine whether the file is infected.

Effectiveness of the technology

Signature scanners require frequent updates to keep their databases of virus signatures current. This updating is necessary to safeguard computer systems against new strains of viruses. When they are properly updated, scanners effectively combat known viruses. However, they are less effective against viruses that change their code each time they infect another computer system.

Activity blockers are generally ineffective against many viruses, including macro viruses that make use of the programming features of common applications such as spreadsheets and word processors. Macro viruses constitute the majority of today's viruses and are encoded within a document as macros—sequences of commands or keyboard strokes that can be stored and then recalled with a single command or keystroke. The macro generally modifies a commonly used function (for example, opening or saving a file) to initiate the effect of the virus. Activity blockers are generally more successful against Trojan horses and worms than they are against viruses.

Heuristic scanners have the primary advantage of being able to detect unknown viruses. Static heuristic scanners, when supplemented with additional programs, can detect behaviors associated with more complex viruses. Dynamic heuristic scanners consume more time and system resources than static heuristic scanners.

File Integrity Checkers

What the technology does

File integrity checkers are software programs that monitor alterations to files that are considered critical either to the organization or the operation of the computer (including changes to the data in the file, permissions, last use, and deletion). Because both authorized and unauthorized activities alter files, file integrity checkers are designed for use with critical files that are not expected to change under normal operating conditions.

File integrity checkers are valuable tools with multiple uses, including

- **Intrusion detection**. File integrity checkers can help detect system compromises, because successful intruders commonly modify system files to provide themselves with a way back into the system (backdoor), hide the attack, and hide their identity.

- **Administration**. Some file integrity checkers have the ability to collect and centralize information from multiple hosts, an ability that assists system administrators in large network environments.

- **Policy enforcement**. System administrators can use file integrity checkers as policy enforcement tools to check whether users or other administrators have made changes that should not have been made or of which the system administrator was not notified.

- **Identification of hardware or software failure**. Integrity checkers might also notice a failing disk. File integrity checkers can also be used to determine if an application had changed files because of design faults.

- **Forensic analysis**. If a system was compromised, a "snapshot" of the system could be taken, which would assist in forensic activities and in prosecuting offenders.

How the technology works

Integrity checkers identify modifications to critical files by comparing the state of a file system against a trusted state, or baseline.[25] The baseline is set to reflect the system's state when it has not been modified in any unauthorized way. First, critical files are encrypted through a one-way hash function, making it nearly impossible to derive the original data from the string.[26] The hash function results in a fixed string of digits, which are stored in a database along with other attributes of the files. The database of the original state of critical files is considered the baseline. To be effective, a baseline should be established immediately after the operating system is installed, before an attacker would have the ability to modify the file system.

After a baseline is created, the integrity checker can then compare the current file system against the baseline. Each critical file's hash is compared with its baseline value. Differences between the hashes indicate that the file has been modified. The user can then determine if any detected changes were unauthorized. If so, the user can take action, for example, assessing the damage and restoring the file or system to a good known state.

Effectiveness of the technology

The effectiveness of file integrity checkers depends on the accuracy of the baseline. Comparisons against a corrupted baseline would result in inaccuracy in identifying modified files. The baseline database should be updated whenever significant changes are made to the system. Care must be taken to ensure that a baseline is not taken of a compromised system.

Also, although they monitor modifications to files, integrity checkers do not prevent changes from occurring. An administrator will notice that the change has occurred only after the integrity checker has been run. Because of the amount of time it can take to check a file system and the

---

[25]The file system is one of the most important parts of an operating system; it stores and manages user data on disk drives and ensures that data read from storage are identical to the data that were originally written. In addition to storing user data in files, the file system creates and manages metadata—information about how, when, and by whom a particular set of data was collected and how the data are formatted

[26]A less secure method uses checksums instead of a hash function.

system resources that requires, these tools are typically run at regularly scheduled intervals.

In addition, integrity checkers may generate false alarms when authorized changes are made to monitored files. Not only can investigating false alarms be time consuming, it could also lead a system administrator to be unwilling to investigate future alarms. As a result, unauthorized changes could go unnoticed.

Cryptography

Cryptography is used to secure transactions by providing ways to ensure data confidentiality (assurance that the information will be protected from unauthorized access), data integrity (assurance that data have not been accidentally or deliberately altered), authentication of the message's originator, electronic certification of data, and nonrepudiation (proof of the integrity and origin of data that can be verified by a third party). Accordingly, cryptography has an important role in protecting information both within a computer system and when information is sent over the Internet and other unprotected communications channels. Encryption is the process of transforming ordinary data (commonly referred to as plaintext) into code form (ciphertext) using a special value known as a key and a mathematical process called an algorithm. Cryptographic algorithms are designed to produce ciphertext that is unintelligible to unauthorized users. Decryption of ciphertext is possible only by using the proper key.

A basic premise in cryptography is that good systems depend only on the secrecy of the key used to perform the operations and not on the secrecy of the algorithm. The algorithms used to perform most cryptographic operations over the Internet are well known. However, because the keys used by these algorithms are kept secret, the process is considered secure.

Cryptographic techniques can be divided into two basic types: secret key cryptography and public key cryptography. Each type has its strengths and

GAO-04-467 Information Security

weaknesses, and systems that utilize both forms are used to take advantage of the strengths of a given type.[27]

- **Secret key, or symmetric, cryptography** employs algorithms in which the key that is used to encrypt the original plaintext message can be calculated from the key that is used to decrypt the ciphertext message, and vice versa. With most symmetric algorithms, the encryption key and the decryption key are the same, and the security of this method rests upon the difficulty of guessing the key. In order to communicate securely, the sender and the receiver must agree on a key and keep the key secret from others. Figure 9 depicts encryption and decryption using a symmetric algorithm. Common symmetric key algorithms include the Triple Digital Encryption Standard (3DES) and the Advanced Encryption Standard (AES).

Figure 9: Encryption and Decryption with a Symmetric Algorithm

Source: GAO analysis.

Public key, or asymmetric, cryptography employs algorithms designed so that the key that is used to encrypt the original plaintext message cannot be calculated from the key that is used to decrypt the ciphertext message. These two keys complement each other in such a way that when one key is used for encryption, only the other key can decrypt the ciphertext. One of these keys is kept private and is known as the private key, while the

---

[27]For additional information on how cryptography works and on some of the issues associated with this technology, see U.S. General Accounting Office, *Information Security: Advances and Remaining Challenges to Adoption of Public Key Infrastructure Technology*, GAO-01-277 (Washington, D.C.: February 26, 2001) and U.S. General Accounting Office, *Information Security: Status of Federal Public Key Infrastructure Activities at Major Federal Departments and Agencies*, GAO-04-157 (Washington, D.C.: December 15, 2003).

GAO-04-467 Information Security

other key is widely publicized and is referred to as the public key. Figure 10 depicts one application of encryption and decryption using a public key algorithm. In this process, the public key is used by others to encrypt a plaintext message, but only a specific person with the corresponding private key can decrypt the ciphertext. For example, if fictional character Bob gives his public key to fictional character Alice, only Bob has the private key that can decrypt a message that Alice has encrypted with his public key. Public key algorithms can also be used in an inverse process, whereby the private key is used to encrypt a message and the public key is made freely available. In this process, those who decrypt the message using the corresponding public key can be confident that the message came from a specific person. For example, if Alice decrypts a message that was encrypted with Bob's private key, she has assurance that the message came from Bob. The most popular public key algorithm is RSA, named for its creators—Rivest, Shamir, and Adleman.

Figure 10: Encryption and Decryption with a Public Key Algorithm

Source: GAO analysis.

Key-based encryption fails if the plaintext or the key is not kept secret from unauthorized users. Such failures often occur not because of a weakness in the technology itself, but rather as a result of poor security policies or practices or malicious insiders.

Secret key cryptography has significant limitations that can make it impractical as a stand-alone solution for securing electronic transactions, especially among large communities of users who may have no pre-established relationships. The most significant limitation is that some means must be devised to securely distribute and manage the keys that are at the heart of the system; such a means is commonly referred to as key management. When many transacting parties are involved, key management may create immense logistical problems and delays. Furthermore, in order to minimize the damage that could be caused by a compromised key, the keys may need to be short-lived and therefore frequently changed, adding to the logistical complexity.

Public key cryptography can address many of the limitations of secret key cryptography regarding key management. There is no need to establish a secure channel or physical delivery services to distribute keys. However, public key cryptography has its own challenges, involving the methods of ensuring that the links between the users and their public keys are initially valid and are constantly maintained. For example, it is impractical and unrealistic to expect that each user will have previously established relationships with all of the other potential users in order to obtain their public keys. Digital certificates (discussed further in this appendix) are one solution to this problem. Furthermore, although a sender can provide confidentiality for a message by encrypting it with the recipient's publicly available encryption key using public key algorithms for large messages, this is computationally time-consuming and could make the whole process unreasonably slow.[28]

Instead, it can be better to combine secret and public key cryptography to provide more efficient and effective means by which a sender can encrypt a document so that only the intended recipient can decrypt it. In this case, the sender of a message would generate a onetime secret encryption key (called a session key) and use it to encrypt the body of her message and then encrypt this session key using the recipient's public key. The encrypted message and the encrypted session key necessary to decrypt the message would then be sent to the recipient. Because the recipient has the information necessary to decrypt the session key, the sender of a message has reasonable assurance in a properly administered system that only the recipient would be able to successfully decrypt the message.

Cryptographic modules implement algorithms that form the building blocks of cryptographic applications. Using a cryptographic system with cryptographic modules that have been approved by an accredited cryptographic certification laboratory (for example, the NIST Cryptographic Module Validation Program) can help provide assurance

---

[28]Most public key cryptographic methods can be used for both encryption and digital signatures. However, certain public key methods—most notably the Digital Signature Algorithm—cannot be used for encryption, but only for digital signatures.

that the system will be effective. However, designing, building, and effectively implementing full-featured cryptographic solutions will remain a difficult challenge because it involves more than just "installing the technology." Encryption technology is effective only if it is an integral part of an effectively enforced information security policy that includes good key management practices. For example, current public key products and implementations suffer from significant interoperability problems, which make it difficult for officials to make decisions about how to develop a public key infrastructure (PKI) that can be used to perform such functions as encrypting data and providing data integrity.[29]

Cryptographic solutions will continue to be used to help provide basic data confidentiality, data integrity, authentication of message originator, electronic certification of data, and nonrepudiation. Technologies that use cryptographic algorithms can be used to encrypt message transmissions so that eavesdroppers cannot determine the contents of a message. Hash technologies use cryptography to provide assurance to a message recipient that the contents of the message have not been altered. For example, operating systems use cryptography to protect passwords. Protocols such as IP Security protocol (IPSec) and Secure Sockets Layer (SSL) use cryptographic technologies for confidential communications. SHA and MD5 are examples of hash technology implementations. Digital signature technologies use cryptography to authenticate the sender of a message. Virtual private networks (VPN) use cryptography to establish a secure communications link across unprotected networks.

Digital Signatures and Certificates

What the technology does

Properly implemented digital signatures use public key cryptography to provide authentication, data integrity, and nonrepudiation for a message or transaction. Just as a physical signature provides assurance that a letter has been written by a specific person, a digital signature confirms the identity of a message's sender. Digital signatures are often used in

---

[29]A PKI is a system of hardware, software, policies, and people that can provide a set of information assurances (identification and authentication, confidentiality, data integrity, and nonrepudiation) that are important in conducting electronic transactions. For more information on PKI, see U.S. General Accounting Office, *Information Security: Advances and Remaining Challenges to Adoption of Public Key Infrastructure Technology*, GAO-01-277 (Washington, D.C.: February 26, 2001).

conjunction with digital certificates. A digital certificate is an electronic credential that guarantees the association between a public key and a specific entity. The most common use of digital certificates is to verify that a user sending a message is who he or she claims to be and to provide the receiver with a means to encode a reply. Certificates can be issued to computer equipment and processes as well as to individuals. For example, companies that do business over the Internet can obtain digital certificates for their computer servers. These certificates are used to authenticate the servers to potential customers, who can then rely on the servers to support the secure exchange of encrypted information, such as passwords and credit card numbers.

How the technology works

The creation of a digital signature is a two-step process based on public key cryptography, as illustrated in figure 11. As previously noted, for performance reasons, public key cryptography is not used to encrypt large amounts of data. Therefore, the first step involves reducing the amount of data that needs to be encrypted. This is typically accomplished by using a cryptographic hash algorithm, which condenses the data into a *message digest*.[30] Then the message digest is encrypted, using the sender's private signing key to create a digital signature. Because the message digest will be different for each signature, each signature will also be unique; if a good hash algorithm is used, it is computationally infeasible to find another message that will generate the same message digest.

---

[30]A hash algorithm compresses the bits of a message to a fixed size. Because any change in the message or the algorithm results in a different value, it is not possible to reverse this process and arrive at the original information.

Figure 11: Creating a Digital Signature

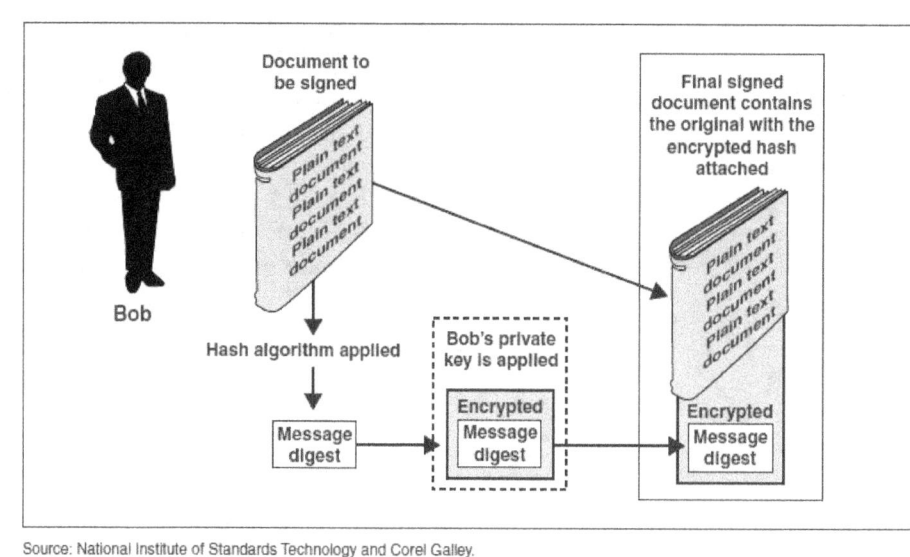

Source: National Institute of Standards Technology and Corel Galley.

For example, if Bob wishes to digitally sign an electronic document, he can use his private key to encrypt the message digest of the document. His public key is freely available, so anyone with access to his public key can decrypt the document. Although this may seem backwards because anyone can read what is encrypted, the fact that Bob's private key is held only by Bob provides the proof that Bob's digital signature is valid.

Figure 12: Verifying a Digital Signature

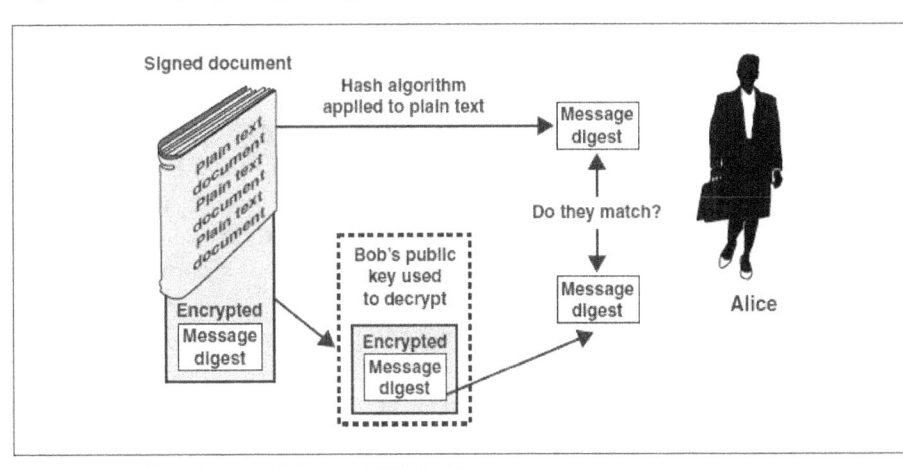

Source: National Institute of Standards Technology and Corel Galley.

Alice (or anyone else wishing to verify the document) can compute the message digest of the document and decrypt the signature using Bob's public key (see fig. 12). Assuming that the message digests match, Alice then has three kinds of security assurance. First, the digital signature ensures that Bob actually signed the document (authentication). Second, it ensures that Bob in fact sent the message (nonrepudiation). And third, because the message digest would have changed if anything in the message had been modified, Alice knows that no one tampered with the contents of the document after Bob signed it (data integrity). Of course, this assumes that (1) Bob has sole control over his private signing key and (2) Alice is sure that the public key she used to validate Bob's messages really belongs to Bob.

Digital certificates address this need to link an individual to his or her public key. A digital certificate is created by placing the individual's name, the individual's public key, and certain other identifying information in a small electronic document that is stored in a directory or other database. Directories may be publicly available repositories kept on servers that act like telephone books in which users can look up others' public keys. The digital certificate itself is created by a trusted third party called a certification authority, which digitally signs the certificate, thus providing assurance that the public key contained in the certificate does indeed belong to the individual named in the certificate. Certification authorities are a main component of a PKI, which uses cryptographic techniques to generate and manage digital certificates.

Effectiveness of the technology

Within an organization, separate key pairs are necessary to support both encryption and digital signatures, and a user's private encryption key should normally be copied to a safe backup location. This provides the organization with the ability to access encrypted data if the user's original private encryption key becomes inaccessible. For example, the organization would have an interest in decrypting data should the private key be destroyed or lost or if the user were fired, incapacitated, or deceased. However, copies of the private keys used for digital signatures should never be made, because they could fall into the wrong hands and be used to forge the owners' signatures.

By linking an individual to his or her public key, digital certificates help to provide assurance that digital signatures are used effectively. However, digital certificates are only as secure as the public key infrastructure that they are based on. For example, if an unauthorized user is able to obtain a private key, the digital certificate could then be compromised. In addition, users of certificates are dependent on certification authorities to verify the digital certificates. If a valid certification authority is not used, or a certification authority makes a mistake or is the victim of a cyber attack, a digital certificate may be ineffective.

Virtual Private Networks

What the technology does

Figure 13: Illustration of a Typical VPN

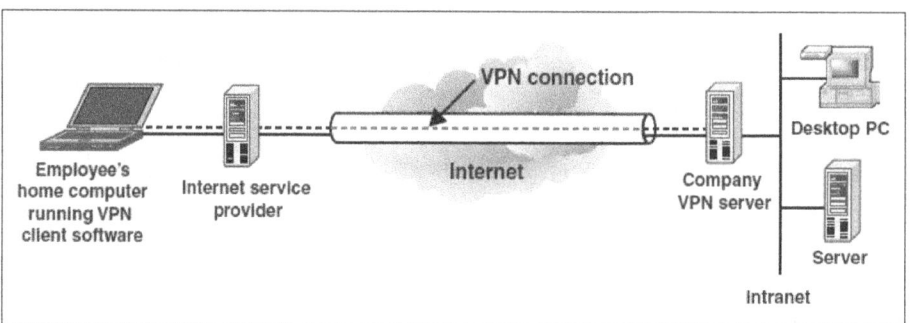

Source: GAO analysis.

A VPN is a private network that is maintained across a shared or public network, such as the Internet, by means of specialized security procedures. VPNs allow organizations or individuals to connect a network between two or more physical locations (for example, field offices and organization headquarters) without incurring the costs of purchasing or leasing dedicated telephone lines or frame relay circuits.[31] (See fig. 13.) Through measures like authentication and data encryption, cryptographic VPNs can establish a secure virtual connection between physical locations.

VPNs can be implemented through hardware, existing firewalls, and stand-alone software applications. To a user, VPNs appear no different than traditional networks and can be used normally whether the user is dialing in from home or accessing a field office from headquarters. VPNs are typically used in intranets and in remote access connections.

- *Intranets* are interlinked private networks within an enterprise that allow information and computer resources to be shared throughout an organization. Some organizations have sensitive data on a LAN that is physically disconnected from the rest of the organization's intranet. This lack of connectivity may cause data on that LAN to be inaccessible to users. A VPN can be used in this situation to allow the sensitive LAN to be physically connected to the intranet—but separated by a VPN server. Only authorized users would be able to establish a VPN connection with the server to gain access to the sensitive LAN, and all communication across the VPN could be encrypted for data confidentiality.

- *Remote access VPNs* simplify the process of remote access, allowing off-site users to connect, via the Internet, to a VPN server at the organization's headquarters. Digital subscriber line (DSL) or cable modem services allow remote VPN users to access the organization's network at speeds comparable to those attained with on-site access.

How the technology works

A VPN works by using shared public networks while maintaining privacy through security procedures and protocols that encrypt communications between two end points. To provide an additional level of security, a VPN can encrypt not only the data, but also the originating and receiving network addresses. There are two main VPN technologies, which differ in

---

[31]Frame relay is a packet-switching protocol for connecting devices on a WAN.

their methods of encrypting data for secure transmission over Internet connections. The first method is based on "tunneling" protocols that encrypt packets at the sending end and decrypt them at the receiving end. This process is commonly referred to as encapsulation, because the original, unsecured packet is placed within another packet that has been secured by encryption. The encapsulated packets are then sent through a "tunnel" that can only be traveled by data that have been properly encrypted. Figure 14 is a depiction of tunneling.

Figure 14: Tunneling Establishes a Virtual Connection

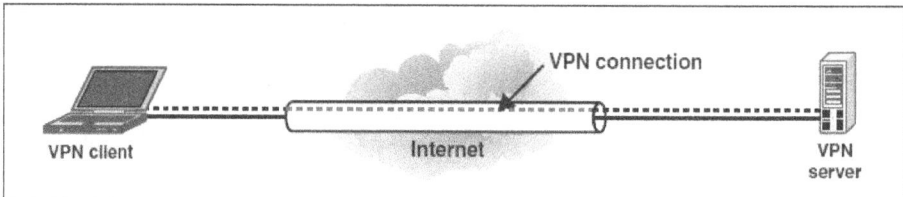

Source: GAO analysis.

A commonly used tunneling protocol is IPSec.[32] IPSec VPNs connect hosts to entire private networks, encrypt IP packets, and ensure that the packets are not deleted, added to, or tampered with during transmission. Because they are based on the IP protocol, IPSec VPNS can secure any IP traffic and can be configured to support any IP-based application.

In addition to tunneling protocols, VPNs can use the SSL protocol, which uses a limited form of public key cryptography. SSL VPNs connect users to services and applications inside private networks, but they secure only the applications' services or data. SSL is a feature of commonly available commercial Web browsers (such as Microsoft's Internet Explorer and America Online's Netscape Navigator), and SSL VPNs use standard browsers instead of the specialized client software that is required by IPSec VPNs.

Effectiveness of the technology

VPNs can be a cost-effective way to secure transmitted data across public networks. However, the cost of implementing IPSec VPNs includes the

---

[32]Other tunneling protocols include Point-to-Point Tunneling Protocol (PPTP) and Layer 2 Tunneling Protocol (L2TP).

installation and configuration of specialized software that is required on every client computer. SSL VPNs use standard Web browsers, eliminating the need for client administration, but the SSL protocol often requires that applications be customized.

In addition, VPNs are only as secure as the computers that are connected to them. Because of the interconnected environment, any unsecured client computer could be used to launch an attack on the network. In particular, VPNs may be susceptible to man-in-the-middle attacks, message replay attacks, and denial-of-service attacks.[33]

Audit and Monitoring

Audit and monitoring technologies can help security administrators to routinely assess computer security, perform investigations during and after an attack, and even recognize an ongoing attack.

We describe four types of audit and monitoring technologies: intrusion detection systems, intrusion prevention systems, security event correlation tools, and computer forensics. Intrusion detection and intrusion prevention systems monitor and analyze events occurring on a system or network and either alert appropriate personnel or prevent an attack from proceeding. Audit logs are produced by many operating systems and software applications. Depending on the configuration of the logging functions, critical activities—such as access to administrator functions—are logged and can be monitored for anomalous activity. Security event correlation tools can help to detect security events and examine logs to determine the method of entry that was used by an attacker and to ascertain the extent of damage that was caused by the attack. Because of the volume of data collected on some systems and networks, these tools can help to consolidate the logs and to identify key information using correlation analysis. Computer forensics involves the identification, preservation, extraction, and documentation of computer-based evidence. Computer forensics tools are used during the

[33]A *man-in-the-middle attack* is one in which the attacker intercepts messages in a public key exchange and then retransmits them, substituting his or her own public key for the requested one, so that the two original parties still appear to be communicating with each other directly. A *message replay attack* is one in which an attacker eavesdrops, obtains a copy of an encrypted message, and then re-uses the message at a later time in an attempt to trick the cryptographic protocol. A *denial-of-service* attack is one in which an attack from a single source overwhelms a target computer with messages, denying access to legitimate users without actually having to compromise the targeted computer.

investigation of a computer crime to identify the perpetrator and the methods that were used to conduct the attack.

Intrusion Detection Systems

What the technology does

An intrusion detection system (IDS) detects inappropriate, incorrect, or anomalous activity that is aimed at disrupting the confidentiality, availability, or integrity of a protected network and its computer systems. An IDS collects information on a network, analyzes the information on the basis of a preconfigured rule set, and then responds to the analysis.

A special type of IDS, known as a *honeypot*, acts as a decoy server or system that gathers information about an attacker or intruder—such as the method of intrusion and the vulnerabilities exploited—in order to improve security methods. To attract attackers, honeypots appear to contain important data, but instead they contain false information. A honeypot can be set up to alert a system administrator of an attack via e-mail or pager, allowing the administrator to ensure that the honeypot is not used as a springboard for future attacks.

How the technology works

There are three common types of IDS, classified by the source of information they use to detect intrusion: network-based, host-based, and application-based.

Network-based IDSs detect attacks by capturing and analyzing network packets. When placed in a network segment, one network-based IDS can monitor the network traffic that affects multiple hosts that are connected to that network segment. Network-based IDSs often consist of a set of single-purpose sensors or hosts, placed at various points in a network. These units monitor network traffic, performing local analysis of that traffic and reporting attacks to a central management console. Because these sensors are limited to running the IDS application only, they can more easily be secured against attacks. Many of these sensors are designed to run in "stealth" mode, making it more difficult for an attacker to detect their presence and location.

Host-based IDSs collect information from within an individual computer system and use that information to detect intrusions. Host-based IDSs can determine exactly which processes and user accounts are involved in a particular attack on the system. Furthermore, unlike network-based IDSs, host-based IDSs can more readily "see" the intended outcome of an attempted attack, because they can directly access and monitor the data files and the system processes that are usually targeted by attacks. Host-based IDSs normally use two types of information sources: operating system audit trails and system logs. Operating system audit trails are usually generated at the innermost level of the operating system; therefore these trails are more detailed and better protected than system logs. Some host-based IDSs are designed to support a centralized IDS management and reporting infrastructure that can allow a single management console to track many hosts. Others generate messages in formats that are compatible with a network management system.

Application-based IDSs are a special subset of host-based IDSs that analyze the events occurring within a specific software application. The most common information sources used by application-based IDSs are the application's transaction log files. Because they directly interface with the application and use application-specific knowledge, application-based IDSs can detect the actions of authorized users who are attempting to exceed their authorization. This is because such problems are more likely to appear in the interaction among the user, the data, and the application.

These IDSs are characterized by four primary qualities: source of information, method of analysis, timing, and response.

IDSs have two primary methods of performing analysis. Signature-based (sometimes referred to as knowledge-based or pattern-based) analysis relies on previous known attacks to detect an attack that is occurring. The IDS analyzes system activity, looking for events that match a predefined pattern of events that describes known attacks. If the analysis of data reveals that an attack is ongoing or that a vulnerability is being exploited, an alarm is generated. Anomaly-based (also referred to as behavior-based) analysis compares the current operation of a system or network against a valid or accepted system behavior. An anomaly-based IDS creates a baseline of normal (valid or accepted) behavior through various collection methods. If the current behavior of the system were not within the normal boundaries of behavior, then it would be interpreted by the IDS as an attack.

IDSs can use either an interval-based or a real-time timing method. The interval-based timing method analyzes the data on a predetermined schedule. This method allows an IDS to collect a large amount of data. The real-time method analyzes and responds to the data as they come in, allowing administrators to respond in real time to attacks.

IDSs can respond to possible attacks using either an active or a passive response strategy. An active response IDS is referred to as an intrusion prevention system (IPS). A passive response IDS will typically generate an alarm for an administrator. The alarm may appear on the administrator's screen and provide the administrator with information such as the type of attack, the location of the attack, the threat level, how it should be responded to, and possibly whether the attack is successful. A passive response IDS relies on a human to take action in response to the alert.

Effectiveness of the technology

IDSs cannot instantaneously detect, report, or respond to an attack when there is a heavy network or processing load. Therefore, IDSs are vulnerable to denial-of-service attacks; a malicious individual could send large amounts of information through a network to overwhelm the IDS, allowing the individual to launch another attack that would then go unnoticed by the IDS. IDSs rely on available attack information, and they are not as effective when protecting against unknown attacks, newly published attacks, or variants of existing attacks. In addition, IDSs are not always able to automatically investigate attacks without human involvement.

The effectiveness of an IDS can be somewhat determined by the number of false positives and false negatives that it generates. A false positive occurs when the IDS alerts that there is an attack occurring, when in fact there is no attack. A false negative occurs when the IDS fails to alert that an attack is occurring. With anomaly-based IDSs, false positives are numerous because of the unpredictable behaviors of users and networks. Administrators must devote a fair amount of time to regularly reviewing the IDS logs and to fine-tuning the IDS to limit the number of false alarms. If excessive false alarms occur, future alarms are increasingly likely to be ignored. Sometimes the IDS may be disabled for the sake of convenience. An attacker could exploit this vulnerability by slowly changing the accepted operation of the system or network recognized by the IDS, allowing for a larger attack to occur at a future time. The attacker could accomplish this by affecting the baseline as it is being created or by later slowly attacking the system so that the baseline moves to a new threshold of accepted behavior. Also, if an anomaly-based IDS is used while an attack is occurring, the normal behavior accepted by the IDS will include behaviors that are characteristic of an attack. Anomaly-based IDSs also take a varying amount of time to compute the valid or accepted behavior, so that for a period of time the IDS will not be an effective method of detecting attacks.

Intrusion Prevention Systems

What the technology does

As we have described, intrusion prevention systems are IDSs with an active response strategy. This means that IPSs not only can detect an intrusive activity, they also can attempt to stop the activity—ideally before it reaches its targets. Intrusion prevention is much more valuable than intrusion detection, because intrusion detection simply observes events without making any effort to stop them. IPSs often combine the best of firewall, intrusion detection, antivirus, and vulnerability assessment technologies. Their focus, however, is on the prevention of detected attacks that might exploit an existing vulnerability in the protected network or host system.

How the technology works

Like IDSs, IPSs are either network-based or host-based. They perform IDS functions and when they detect an intrusion, take action such as blocking the network traffic to prevent the attack from proceeding. Network-based IPSs may simply monitor the network traffic or they may actually be "in line," which means that activity must pass through them. For example, an IPS includes a network-based IDS that is integrated with a firewall and a host-based IDS that integrates the detection and prevention functionalities into the kernel of the operating system. Network-based IPSs thoroughly inspect data traffic, typically using specialized hardware to compensate for the processing overhead that inspection consumes.

IPSs actively respond to possible attacks by collecting additional information, changing the current environment, and taking action against the intruder. One of their common responses is to adjust firewall rules to block the offending network traffic. If an IPS responds to an attack by taking action against the intruder (a mode of operation commonly referred to as attack-back or strike-back), it may launch a series of attacks against the attacker. In another aggressive response, called trace-back, the IPS attempts to find the source of the attack.

Effectiveness of the technology

Intrusion prevention systems are the logical evolution of intrusion detection systems. Instead of dealing with the constant warning alarms of IDSs, IPSs can prevent attacks by blocking suspicious network traffic. A key value of some IPSs is their ability to "learn" what constitutes acceptable behavior and to halt activity that is not based on rules that were generated during the learning, or profiling, stage.

Network-based IPSs offer in-line monitoring of data streams throughout the network and provide the capability to prevent intrusion attempts. Host-based IPSs allow systems and applications to be configured individually, preventing attacks against the operating system or applications. These IPSs are suitable measures to help guard unpatched and exploitable systems against attacks, but they require substantial user administration.

Unfortunately, IPSs are susceptible to errors in detecting intrusions. If the detection of incidents is not accurate, then an IPS may block legitimate activities that are incorrectly classified as malicious. Any organization that wants to utilize intrusion prevention should pay particular attention to detection accuracy when selecting a product.

Users of IPSs also face the challenge of maintaining a database of recent attack signatures so that systems can be guarded against recent attack strategies. Furthermore, IPSs cause bottlenecks in network traffic, reducing throughput across the network.

Security Event Correlation Tools

What the technology does

Security event correlation tools collect logs, or lists of actions that have occurred, from operating systems, firewalls, applications, IDSs, and other network devices. Then the correlation tools analyze the logs in real time, discern whether an attack has occurred, and respond to a security incident.

Review and analysis of logs can provide a dynamic picture of ongoing system activities that can be used to verify that the system is operating according to the organization's policies. Analyzing a single device's logs is insufficient to gain a full understand of all system activity, but the size, number, and difficulty of reading through every tool's log files is a daunting task for an administrator. Security event correlation tools address the need for an administrator to investigate an attack in a real-time setting, through analysis and correlation of all the different IDS, firewall, and server logs. Automated audit tools provide a means to significantly reduce the required review time, and they will print reports (predefined and customized) that summarize the log contents from a set of specific activities (see fig. 15).

Figure 15: Typical Operation of Security Event Correlation Tools

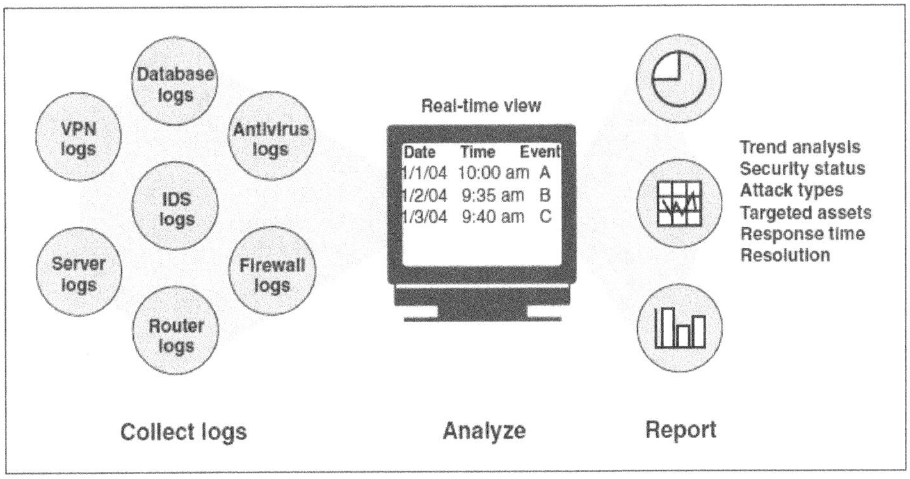

How the technology works

Security event correlation tools first consolidate the log files from various sources, such as operating systems, firewalls, applications, IDSs, antivirus programs, servers, and virtual private networks. Often, the logs from the various sources come in a variety of proprietary formats that make comparisons difficult. As part of the consolidation process, security event correlation tools normalize the logs into a standard format—for example, Extensible Markup Language (commonly referred to as XML).[34] After the normalization process, unnecessary data can be eliminated in order to decrease the chance of errors.

---

[34]XML is a flexible, nonproprietary set of standards for tagging information so that it can be transmitted over a network such as the Internet and be readily interpreted by disparate computer systems.

GAO-04-467 Information Security

The normalized logs are then compared (or correlated) to determine whether attacks have occurred. A variety of correlation methods can be used, including sophisticated pattern-based analysis, which can identify similar activity on various logs that have originated from an attack. For example, an IDS might not raise a flag if a single port was being scanned. However, if that port were being scanned on multiple systems, that activity might indicate an attack. By consolidating the logs from the various IDSs, correlation tools may detect this type of attack. A second method of analysis is called *anomaly detection*. In this method, a baseline of normal user activity is taken, and logged activities are compared against this baseline. Abnormal activity can then be interpreted as potentially indicating an attack. Another correlation method considers the significance of the logged event, which can be calculated as the probability that the attack would have succeeded.

If an attack is detected, the tools can then respond either passively or actively. A passive response means that no action is taken by the tool to stop the threat directly. For example, notifications can be sent to system administrators via pagers or e-mail, incidents can be logged, and IP addresses can be added to intruder or asset watch lists. An active response is an automated action taken by the tool to mitigate the risk. For example, one active response is to block the attack through interfaces with firewalls or routers.

Effectiveness of the technology

Correlation tools are limited in their ability to interface with numerous security products; they may not be able to collect and correlate logs from certain products. In addition, these tools rely on the sufficiency and accuracy of the logs, and they cannot detect attacks that have bypassed the various security devices, such as the firewall and IDS. If an attacker were able to compromise the logs, then the security event correlation tool could be analyzing false information. Encryption and authentication to ensure the security and integrity of the data may mitigate this risk.

Computer Forensics Tools

What the technology does

Computer forensics tools are used to identify, preserve, extract, and document computer-based evidence. They can identify passwords, log-ons, and other information in files that have been deleted, encrypted, or damaged. During the investigation of a computer crime, these tools are

GAO-04-467 Information Security

used to determine the perpetrator and the methods that were used to conduct the attack.

There are two main categories of computer forensics tools: (1) evidence preservation and collection tools, which prevent the accidental or deliberate modification of computer-related evidence and create a logical or physical copy of the original evidence, and (2) analysis tools, which provide data recovery and discovery functions. A few commercially available computer forensics products incorporate features of both categories and claim to provide a complete suite of forensics tools.

How the technology works

Evidence Preservation and Collection Tools

Write protection and disk-imaging software are used to preserve and copy computer evidence while preserving its integrity.

There are several techniques that are used by write protection software, which prevents or disables a user's attempts to modify data (or perform the "write" operation) on a computer's hard drive or on other computer media. In one method, the write protection software attempts to gain exclusive access to the media through mechanisms specific to the operating system. If exclusive access can be gained, all other software applications will be prevented from accessing and modifying the locked media. Another method utilizes a separate software component that is installed as part of the operating system and is loaded when the operating system starts (and before any other application can execute).

Disk imaging is a process that attempts to copy every bit of data from one physical computer medium to another, similar medium. This type of duplication is known as a physical disk copy, and it involves copying all data, including files, file names, and data that are not associated with a file. Disk-imaging tools may also perform varying degrees of integrity checking to verify that all data have been copied without error or alteration. The most common technique used to verify data integrity is a digital signature or a checksum algorithm.

Analysis Tools

These tools can recover deleted files by taking advantage of a common technique that is typically employed by commercial operating systems. When a user deletes a file from a computer medium (such as a floppy disk or hard drive), many operating systems do not destroy the data contained in the files. Instead, the space occupied by the deleted file is marked as available, or unallocated, so it can be reused as new files are created. The unallocated data contained in those deleted files may still remain on the medium. Analysis tools that recover unallocated data examine a specific structure and organization of information (called a file system) as it is stored on computer media. Because common operating systems maintain data in unique file systems that vary greatly, these analysis tools are typically designed for a specific file system.

Other analysis tools examine text files to identify the occurrence and frequency of specific words or patterns. They can generate a word index by creating a database of every word or delimited string that is contained within a single file, a collection of files, or an entire medium. They can also search multiple files or entire media for the occurrence of specified strings or words, as well as perform advanced searches using Boolean expressions.[35] Some tools have the capability to perform *fuzzy logic* searches, which search for derivatives of a word, related words, and misspelled words. For example, when searching for files containing the word "bomb," files that contain "bombed," "explosive," or "bommb" may also be considered as matches.

Other analysis tools identify files by their type or individual identity, a method that can reduce the volume of data that an investigator must analyze. File type identification is based on a file signature—a unique sequence of values stored within a file that may be as short as 2 characters or longer than 12 characters. The longer the sequence, the greater the uniqueness of the signature and the less likely it is that a file will be mislabeled. Individual file identification is also signature-based, but the method calculates a signature over an entire file or data unit. One approach utilizes a representation that is both efficient in storage requirements and reliable in terms of its uniqueness, such as a hashing algorithm.

---

[35]In Boolean searches, an "and" operator between two words or other values (for example, "pear AND apple") means one is searching for documents containing both of the words or values, not just one of them. An "or" operator between two words or other values (for example, "pear OR apple") means one is searching for documents containing either of the words.

GAO-04-467 Information Security

Effectiveness of the technology

There are many different automated tools that are routinely used by law enforcement organizations to assist in the investigation of crimes involving computers. These tools are employed to generate critical evidence that is used in criminal cases. However, there are no standards or recognized tests by which to judge the validity of the results produced by these tools. Computer forensics tools must meet the same standards that are applied to all forensic sciences, including formal testable theories, peer-reviewed methodologies and tools, and replicable empirical research. Failing to apply standards may result in contaminating or losing critical evidence. It is important to obtain legal advice and consult with law enforcement officials before undertaking any forensic activities in situations where criminal or civil investigation or litigation is a potential outcome.

Configuration Management and Assurance

Configuration management and assurance technologies help security administrators to view and change the security settings on their hosts and networks, verify the correctness of the security settings, and maintain operations in a secure fashion under duress. Technologies that assist configuration management and assurance include policy enforcement tools, network management tools, continuity of operations tools, scanners for testing and auditing security, and patch management tools.

Policy enforcement tools help administrators define and ensure compliance with a set of security rules and configurations, such as a password policy, access to systems and files, and desktop and server configurations. Management and administration tools are used to maintain networks and systems. These tools incorporate functions that facilitate central monitoring of the security posture of networks and systems. Network management tools obtain status data from network components, make configuration changes, and alert network managers to problems.

To provide continuity of operations, there are secure backup tools that can restore system functionality and data in the event of a disruption. These products are used to account for naturally occurring problems, such as power outages, and are now also being applied to help address problems resulting from malicious cyber attacks. Tools are also available to help systems and networks continue to perform during an attack.

Scanners are common testing and audit tools that are used to identify vulnerabilities in networks and systems. As part of proactive security testing, scanners are available that can be used to probe modems, Internet ports, databases, wireless access points, and Web pages and applications. These tools often incorporate the capability to monitor the security posture of the networks and systems by testing and auditing their security configurations.

Patch management tools help system administrators with the process of acquiring, testing, and applying fixes to operating systems and applications. Software vendors typically provide these fixes to correct known vulnerabilities in their software.

Policy Enforcement Applications

What the technology does

Policy enforcement technologies allow system administrators to perform centralized monitoring of compliance with an organization's security policies.[36] These tools examine desktop and server configurations that define authorized access to specified devices and compare these settings against a baseline policy. They typically provide multilevel reports on computer configurations, and some products have the capability to fix various identified problems. They also provide information that can help centralized administrators more effectively use other security technologies, such as access control and security event and correlation tools.

How the technology works

Policy enforcement tools generally have four main functions:

Policy definition. These tools can help establish baseline policy settings. Policies can include features like minimum password requirements and user and group rights to specific applications. Some products include policy templates that can be customized and distributed to users for review and signatures.

Compliance checking. After a security policy has been defined, these tools can compare current system configurations with the baseline settings. Compliance can be monitored across multiple administrative

---

[36]Policy is defined as a set of configurations and access controls that affect the overall security stance of a user, group, device, or application.

domains and operating systems from a central management console. For example, compliance checking could include testing for a particular setting in multiple systems' configuration files, checking the audit configuration on a subset of computers, or checking that console password settings fit the policies of the organization (for example, using the correct number of characters in a password, using alphanumeric characters, and periodically changing passwords). The tools often allow customized checks to be defined.

Reporting. Basic reporting templates are generally included with these tools, such as templates for configurations, user accounts, access controls, and software patch levels. In addition, users can often customize reports and create ad hoc queries for specific information on particular computers. These reports can consolidate information, such as which users have not recently logged on to a system and which computers are running unpatched applications. The reports can be tailored differently for security personnel and management.

Remediation. Some policy enforcement tools allow problems that have been discovered to be fixed proactively. For example, if the latest security software patch for a particular application has not been installed, some tools automatically download patches from a vendor's Web site and either alert an administrator or install the patches directly onto the system.

Effectiveness of the technology

Policy enforcement software can provide for centralized monitoring, control, and enforcement. However, the software's effectiveness is largely governed by the security policies of the organization. These tools can only assist in monitoring and enforcing those policies that organizations choose to implement. As a result, they can be only as good as the policies that the organization defines. In addition, some policy enforcement tools do not work on all operating systems, and installation and configuration can be arduous.

Network Management

What the technology does

Network management is the ability to control and monitor a computer network from a central location. Network management systems consist of software and dedicated computer hardware that view the entire network as a unified architecture in order to obtain status data from network components, make configuration changes, and alert network managers to problems. The International Organization for Standardization defines a conceptual model for describing the five key functional areas of network management (and the main functions of network management systems):

- **Fault management** identifies problems in nodes, the network, and the network's operation to determine their causes and to take remedial action.

- **Configuration management** monitors network configuration information so that the effects of specific hardware and software can be managed and tracked.

- **Accounting management** measures network utilization by individual users or groups in order to provide billing information, regulate users or groups, and help keep network performance at an acceptable level.

- **Performance management** measures various aspects of network performance, including gathering and analyzing statistical system data so that performance may be maintained at an acceptable level.

- **Security management** controls access to network resources by limiting access to network resources, and by providing notification of security breaches and attempts, so that information cannot be obtained without authorization.

How the technology works

A network management system typically consists of managed devices (the network hosts); software agents, which communicate information about the managed devices; a network management application, which gathers and processes information from agents; and a network management station, which allows an operator to view a graphical representation of the network, control managed devices on the network, and program the network management application. Figure 16 is an example of a typical network management architecture.

Figure 16: Typical Network Management Architecture

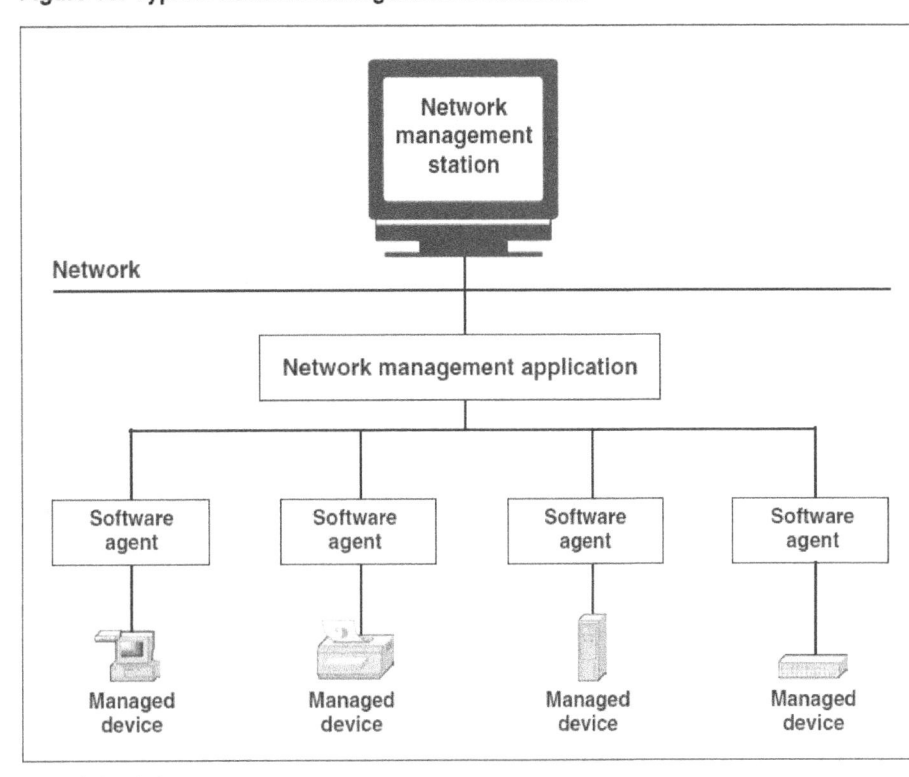

Source: GAO analysis.

The network management station receives and processes events from network elements and acts as the main console for network operations. The network management station displays a graphical network map that highlights the operational states of critical network devices such as routers and switches. Each network device is represented by a graphical element on the management station's console, and different colors are used to represent the current operational status of network devices, based on status notifications sent by the devices. These notifications (usually called events) are placed in a log file.

The functionality of network management software (network management applications and agents) depends on the particular network management protocol that the software is based on. Most systems use open protocols. However, some network management software is based upon vendor-specific proprietary protocols. The two most common network management protocols are the Simple Network Management Protocol (SNMP) and Common Management Information Protocol (CMIP). SNMP is widely used in most LAN environments. CMIP is used in telecommunication environments, where networks tend to be large and complex.

Effectiveness of the technology

Network management systems can be quite expensive and they are often complex. The complexity is primarily in the network management protocols and data structures that are associated with the network management information. Also, these systems require personnel with the specialized training to effectively configure, maintain, and operate the network management system.

Many network management systems cannot support network devices that use vendor-specific protocols.

Continuity-of-Operations Tools

What the technology does

Continuity-of-operations tools provide a complete backup infrastructure to keep the enterprise's data resources online and available at multiple locations in case of an emergency or planned maintenance, such as system or software upgrading. They maintain operational continuity of the storage devices and host and database levels. Continuity-of-operations tools include *high-availability systems*, which link two or more computers together to provide continuous access to data through systems redundancy (known as clustering); *journaling file systems*, which maintain specific information about data to avoid file system errors and corruption; *load-balancing* technology, which distributes traffic efficiently among network servers so that no individual server is overburdened; and *redundant array of independent disk* (RAID) technology, which allows two or more hard drives to work in concert for increased fault tolerance and improved performance. [37]

---

[37]Fault tolerance is the ability of a system to respond gracefully to an unexpected hardware or software failure.

How the technology works

High-availability systems use *clustering*, which refers to two or more
servers set up in such a way that if an application running on one server
fails, it can then be automatically restarted or recovered on another server.
This is referred to as *fail over* from one server or node in the cluster to
another. High-availability systems utilize fail-over operations to
automatically switch to a standby database, server, or network if the
primary system fails or is temporarily shut down for servicing. Some high-
availability systems can also perform remote backups, remote mutual
takeovers, concurrent access operations, and remote system recoveries.
These functions are described below:

- In a *remote backup*, a remote geographic site is designated as a hot
  backup site that is live and ready to take over the current workload. This
  backup site includes hardware, system, and application software and
  application data and files. In the event of a failure, the failed site's
  application workload automatically moves to the remote hot backup site.

- In a *remote mutual takeover,* geographically separated system sites are
  designated as hot backups for each other. Should either site experience a
  failure, the other acts as a hot backup and automatically takes over the
  designated application workload of the failed site. Two different
  workloads running at two different sites are protected.

- In *concurrent access,* systems at both sites are concurrently updating the
  same database.

- In *remote system recovery,* data can be resynchronized, and a failed
  system that has been restored to operation can be reintegrated with the
  remote hot backup. In a process known as file mirroring, the failed system
  is updated with current application data and files that were processed by
  the backup system after the failed system ceased operations. Upon
  completing restoration of an up-to-date data and file mirror, the high-
  availability system will resume synchronized system operations, including
  the mirroring of real-time data and files between the system sites. This can
  occur while the remote backup is in use.

A *journaling file system* ensures that the data on a disk have been restored
to their prefailure configuration. It also recovers unsaved data and stores
them in their intended locations (had the computer not failed), making the
journaling file system an important feature for mission-critical
applications. A journaling file system transaction treats a sequence of
changes as a single operation and tracks changes to file system metadata

and user data. The transaction guarantees that either all or none of the file system updates are done.

For example, the process of creating a new file modifies several metadata values. Before the file system makes those changes, it creates a transaction to record the intended changes. Once the transaction has been recorded on disk, the file system modifies the metadata and the transaction that are stored on the journaling file system. In the event of a system failure, the file system is restored to a consistent state by repeating the transactions listed in the journal. Rather than examining all metadata, the file system inspects only those portions of the metadata that have recently changed.

Load-balancing technology distributes processing and communications activity evenly across a computer network by transferring the tasks from heavily loaded processors to the ones with lighter loads. Load-balancing decisions are based on three policies: an information policy, which specifies the amount of load information to be made available; a transfer policy, which specifies the current workload of the host and the size of the job; and a placement policy, which specifies proper allocation of processes to the different computer processors.

RAID systems provide large amounts of storage by making the data on many smalls disks readily available to file servers, host computers, or the network as a single unit (known as an *array*). The design of the array of disks is an important determinant of performance and data availability in a RAID system. In addition to deploying an array of disks, RAID systems include a controller—an intelligent electronic device that routes, buffers, and manages data flow between the host computer and the network array of disks. RAID controllers can organize data on the disks in several ways in order to optimize the performance and reliability of the system for different types of applications. RAID can also be implemented in software.

Effectiveness of the technology

Continuity-of-operations technologies can help an agency increase the availability of its mission-critical applications. Some of the technologies—such as RAID and journaling file systems—increase the ability of a single server to survive a number of failures. For many agencies, the combination of RAID, journaling file system, and redundant power supply can provide adequate protection against disruptions.

Organizations that cannot tolerate an application outage of more than a few minutes may deploy a high-availability system that uses clustering. Clustering has a proven track record as a good solution for increasing application availability. However, clustering is expensive because it requires additional hardware and clustering software, and it is more complex to manage than a single system.

Scanners

What the technology does

Scanners help to identify a network's or a system's security vulnerabilities. There are a variety of scanning tools, including port scanners, vulnerability scanners, and modem scanners.[38]

Port scanners are used to map networks and identify the services running on each host by detecting open TCP and user datagram protocol (UDP) ports. Vulnerability scanners are used to identify vulnerabilities on computer hosts and networks and to make use of the results that were generated by a port scanner. These tools have reporting features to list the vulnerabilities that they identified, and may provide instructions on how to reduce or eliminate the vulnerability. Many scanners are now equipped to automatically fix selected vulnerabilities.

Modem scanners, also known as *war dialers*, are programs that identify phone numbers that can successfully make a connection with a computer modem. Unauthorized modems can provide a means to bypass most or all of the security measures in place to stop unauthorized users from accessing a network—such as firewalls and intrusion detection systems.

How the technology works

Port scanners use methods known as *ping sweeps* and *port scans* to map networks and identify services that are in use. Ping sweeps are considered the most basic technique for scanning a network. A ping sweep determines which range of IP addresses map to computers that are turned on by sending communication requests (known as Internet Control Message Protocol [ICMP] ECHO requests) to multiple IP addresses. If a computer at

---

[38]Other scanning tools include database scanners, Web application scanners, and wireless packet analyzers.

a target address is turned on, it will return a specific ICMP ECHO reply. In port scanning, the scanner sends a message to a specific port on a target computer and waits for a response. The responses to a scan can allow the scanner to determine (1) which ports are open and (2) the operating system the computer is running (certain port scans only work on certain operating systems). The type of message that is sent and the information the scanner receives can distinguish the various types of port scans.

Vulnerability scanners are software applications that can be used to identify vulnerabilities on computer hosts and networks. Host-based scanners must be installed on each host to be tested, and they typically require administrative-level access to operate. Network-based scanners operate on an organization's network and identify vulnerabilities on multiple computers. Whether host-based or network-based, vulnerability scanners automatically identify a host's operating system and active applications; they then compare these with the scanners' database of known vulnerabilities. Vulnerability scanners employ large databases of known vulnerabilities to identify the vulnerabilities that are associated with commonly used operating systems and applications. When a match is found, the scanner will alert the operator to a possible vulnerability. Figure 17 shows a sample screen from a vulnerability scanner.

Figure 17: Example of a Vulnerability Scanner Screen

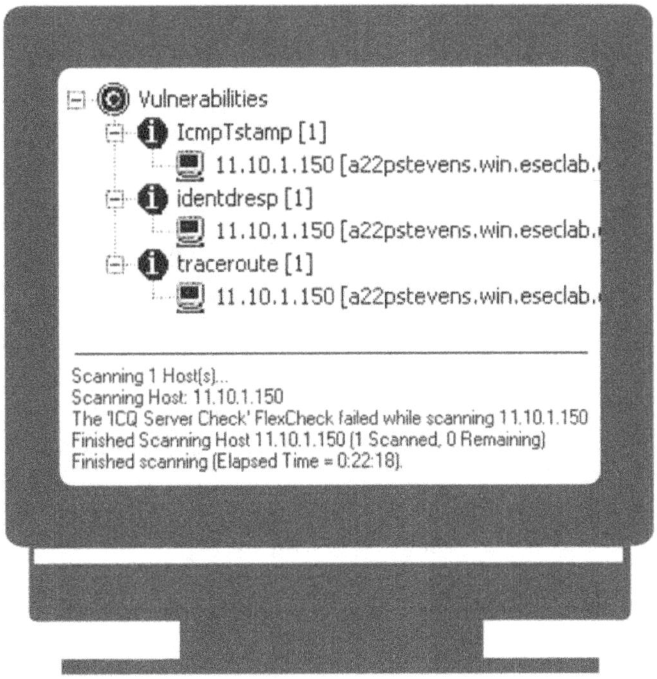

Source: GAO.

Modem scanners are software programs that automatically dial a defined range of phone numbers and track successful connections in a database. Some modem scanners can also identify the particular operating system running on the computer, and they may be configured to attempt to gain access to the system by running through a predetermined list of common user names and passwords.

Effectiveness of the technology

Port-scanning applications have the capability to scan a large number of hosts, but they do not directly identify known vulnerabilities. However, some vulnerability scanners can perform a port scan to target specific network hosts for vulnerability scanning. Vulnerability scanners can identify vulnerabilities and suggest how to fix them, but they may not themselves have the capability to fix all identified vulnerabilities. They have been known to generate false positives (i.e., detecting a vulnerability that does not exist) and false negatives (i.e., not detecting a vulnerability that does exist). While false positives are irrelevant warnings that can be ignored, false negatives can result in overlooking critical security

GAO-04-467 Information Security

vulnerabilities. Also, their effectiveness is linked to the quality of the database of known vulnerabilities; if the database is not up to date, vulnerability scanners might not identify newly discovered vulnerabilities.

Patch Management

What the technology does

Patch management tools automate the otherwise manual process of acquiring, testing, and applying patches to multiple computer systems.[39] These tools can be either stand-alone patch management products or the patch component of systems management products. Patch management tools are used to identify missing patches on each system, deploy patches to a single or to multiple computers, and generate reports to track the status of a patch across a number of computers. Some tools offer customized features, including automated inventorying and immediate notification of new patches. While patch management tools primarily support the Windows operating system, they are expanding to support multiple platforms.

How the technology works

Patch management tools have various system requirements, such as specific applications, servers, and service pack levels, depending on the tool selected. Patch management tools can be either *scanner-based (non-agent)* or *agent-based*. Agent-based tools place small programs, or agents, on each computer. The agents periodically poll a patch database—a server on a network—for new updates and apply the patches pushed out by the administrator. This architecture allows for either the client or the server to initiate communications, which means that individual computers can either query the patch database or allow the server to perform a scan to determine their configuration status. Some patch management vendors have contractual agreements with software vendors to receive pre-notification of vulnerabilities and related patches before they are publicly released. These patch management vendors test the patch before it is made available at a designated location (for example, a server), where it can be automatically downloaded for deployment. The agents will then install the patches for the systems meeting the patch requirements.

---

[39]A patch is an upgrade designed to fix a serious flaw (that is, a vulnerability) in a piece of software and is typically developed and distributed as a replacement for or an insertion in compiled code.

GAO-04-467 Information Security

Scanner-based tools can scan the computers on a network according to provided criteria, such as domain or IP range, to determine their configurations. The server initiates communication with the client by logging in and querying each machine as a domain or local administrator. Patches are downloaded from the vendor's Web site and stored at a designated location to be installed to the target machine.

Most tools also have built-in knowledge repositories that compare the systems' established versions against lists that contain the latest vulnerabilities and notifications of fixes. They also have the capability to make recommendations on which patches to deploy on given machines. Additionally, these tools can analyze whether the relevant patch has been deployed to all affected systems. Many tools can also prioritize patch deployment and dependencies on each system. This capability can allow for logical grouping of target machines in order to streamline the patch installation process.

Effectiveness of the technology

While patch management tools can automate patch delivery, it is still necessary to determine whether a particular patch is appropriate to apply. In addition, patches may need to be tested against the organization's specific systems configurations. The complexity of the organization's enterprise architecture determines the difficulty of this task. Also, some of these tools are not consistently accurate in that they will incorrectly report that a patch is missing when it has actually been installed (that is, a false negative) or report that patches have been installed on unpatched systems (that is, a false positive). Furthermore, the automated distribution of patches may be a potential security exposure, because patches are a potential entry point into an organization's infrastructure.

Agent-based products can reduce network traffic, because the processing and analysis are offloaded to the target system and are not done on the network. In this kind of implementation, the work is performed at the client, which offloads the processing and analysis to the individual computers and saves the data until it needs to report to the central server. Agent-based products, however, require more maintenance, deployment, and labor costs because of their distributed architecture. Additionally, the task of installing agents on each machine requires more work on the front end. Agent-based tools are better suited for larger networks because they can provide a real-time network view.

Scanner-based tools are easier and faster to deploy and do not present distributive management concerns. However, they can significantly increase network traffic, because tests and communications travel over the network whenever a scan is requested. Additionally, computers that are not connected to the network at the time scans are performed are not accounted for. Because of these shortcomings, scanner-based tools are recommended only for smaller, static networks.

Implementation Considerations Should Be Addressed

The selection and effective implementation of cybersecurity technologies require adequate consideration of a number of key factors, including

- implementing technologies through a layered, defense-in-depth strategy;

- considering the agency's unique IT infrastructure when selecting technologies;

- utilizing results of independent testing when assessing the technologies' capabilities;

- training staff on the secure implementation and utilization of these technologies; and

- ensuring that the technologies are securely configured.

Implementing Multiple Technologies Provides Defense in Depth

According to security experts, a best practice for protecting systems against cyber attacks is for agencies to build successive layers of defense mechanisms at strategic points in their IT infrastructures. This approach, commonly referred to as *defense in depth*, entails implementing a series of protective mechanisms such that if one mechanism fails to thwart an attack, another will provide a backup defense. Because of the interconnectivity of an agency's IT infrastructure, each of the components represents a potential point of vulnerability to cyber attacks. Moreover, because there is a wide variety of attack methods available to exploit these vulnerabilities and there are many potential attackers, both external and internal, no single technical solution can successfully protect the information systems of federal agencies from potential cyber attacks. By utilizing the strategy of defense in depth, agencies can reduce the risk of a successful cyber attack. For example, multiple firewalls could be deployed to prevent both outsiders and trusted insiders from gaining unauthorized access to systems: one firewall could be deployed at the network's Internet connection to control access to and from the Internet, while another firewall could be deployed between WANs and LANs to limit employee access.

In addition to deploying a series of similar security technologies at multiple layers, deploying diverse technologies at different layers also mitigates the risk of successful cyber attacks. Because cybersecurity technology products have different capabilities and inherent limitations, it is only a matter of time before an adversary will find an exploitable vulnerability. If several different technologies are deployed between the adversary and the targeted system, the adversary must overcome the unique obstacle presented by each of the technologies. For example, firewalls and intrusion detection technologies can be deployed to defend against attacks from the Internet, and antivirus software can be utilized to provide integrity protection for data transmitted over the network. In this way, defense in depth can be effectively implemented through multiple security measures among hosts, LANs and WANs, and the Internet.

Defense in depth also entails implementing an appropriate network configuration, which can in turn affect the selection and implementation of cybersecurity technologies. For example, configuring the agency's network to channel Internet access through a limited number of connections improves security by reducing the number of points that can be attacked from the Internet. At the same time, the agency can focus technology solutions and attention on protecting and monitoring the limited number of connections for unauthorized access attempts.

Figure 18 depicts how applying a layered approach to security through deploying both similar and diverse cybersecurity technologies at multiple layers can deflect different types of attacks.

Figure 18: Layered Approach to Network Security

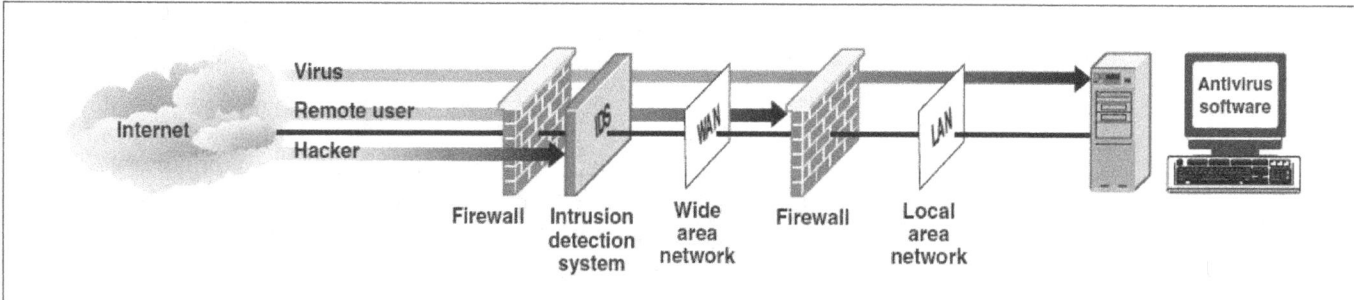

Product Selection Depends on Security Infrastructure

The selection of multiple technologies can be made in the context of the overall security infrastructure and not aimed solely at specific components of the system or the network. When selecting cybersecurity technologies, it is important to consider the effects of the technologies and processes on the agency's mission. For example, if a security mechanism makes a process difficult or inconvenient, users may try to bypass the process or conduct their business in different ways. Agencies can balance their use of security technologies against the level of service that the computers and network must provide. Products that are appropriate for an agency will vary based on a number of factors, such as the agency's specific IT infrastructure, security objectives, costs, performance requirements, schedule constraints, and operational constraints. Agencies may choose to perform a cost-benefit analysis, including a life-cycle cost estimate for each product and a calculation of the benefits associated with each product that can be identified in terms of dollar savings or cost avoidance.

NIST has developed a guide for use by federal agencies in selecting cybersecurity products.[40] This guide builds upon previous NIST guidance for the acquisition and use of security-related products as well as

---

[40]National Institute of Standards and Technology, *Guide to Selecting Information Technology Security Products*, NIST Special Publication 800-36 (October 2003).

GAO-04-467 Information Security

numerous other NIST publications dedicated to individual cybersecurity technologies. [41]

The Capabilities of Security Technologies Can Be Independently Tested and Evaluated

Instead of relying on vendors' claims regarding the capabilities of their products, agencies can procure technologies that have been independently tested and evaluated, to ensure that the products meet security standards. By doing so, agencies may gain greater confidence that the products work as advertised by the vendor. Testing also provides a way to demonstrate that the product complies with security requirements.

Two prominent security testing and evaluation programs are in place to assess the security features and assurances of commercial off-the-shelf (COTS) products. The National Information Assurance Partnership (NIAP) is a collaborative effort by NIST and NSA to produce comprehensive security requirements and security specifications for technologies that will be used to secure IT systems. NIAP licenses and approves laboratories to evaluate security technologies against the Common Criteria, a unified set of international security standards. Some of the product types they have validated are firewalls, VPNs, antivirus software, and IDSs.[42] National Information Assurance Acquisition Policy requires all IT security products purchased by the federal government for systems that enter, process, store, display, or transmit national security information to be Common Criteria–certified.[43]

In addition to supporting Common Criteria certification of products, NIST operates the Cryptographic Module Validation Program, which uses independent, accredited, private-sector laboratories to perform security testing of cryptographic modules for conformance to Federal Information Processing Standards Publication (FIPS) 140-2—*Security Requirements for Cryptographic Modules*—and related federal cryptographic algorithms standards. When agencies have determined that they need to protect

---

[41]National Institute of Standards and Technology, *Guidlines to Federal Agencies on Security Assurance and Acquisition/Use of Tested/Evaluated Products*, NIST Special Publication 800-23 (August 2000).

[42]The full list of validated products can be found at the NIAP Web site: http://niap.nist.gov/.

[43]Committee on National Security Systems, National Security Telecommunications and Information Systems Security Policy (NSTISSP) No. 11, Subject: National Policy Governing the Acquisition of Information Assurance (IA) and IA-Enabled Information Technology (IT) Products (January 2000, revised June 2003).

GAO-04-467 Information Security

information via cryptographic means, they are required by FIPS 140-2 to select only from validated cryptographic modules.

The results of such evaluations can help agencies decide whether an evaluated product fulfils their security needs. Agencies can also use available evaluation results to compare different products. This is a value-added for technologies such as computer forensics tools that currently have no standards against which to test.

Well-Trained Staff Are Essential

FISMA recognizes that technology and people must work together to implement policies, processes, and procedures that serve as countermeasures to identified risks. Breaches in security resulting from human error are more likely to occur if personnel do not understand the risks and the policies that have been put in place to mitigate them. Training is an essential component of a security management program. Personnel who are trained to exercise good judgment in following security procedures can successfully mitigate vulnerabilities. For example, an agency that has identified a risk of external intruders gaining access to a sensitive system may implement an access policy to mitigate this risk. The policy may specify that all external connections to the agency network must pass through a firewall. However, unless users of the sensitive system understand the risks of not complying with the access policy, they may unknowingly activate rogue modems that allow intruders to bypass the firewall and gain access.

In addition, having the best available security technology cannot ensure protection if people have not been trained in how to use it properly. Agencies need people who understand the risks and have the necessary technological expertise to deploy technologies so as to maximize their effectiveness. Training is particularly essential if the technology requires personnel to master certain knowledge and skills to securely implement it.

Proper Technology Configuration Is Critical

To effectively implement cybersecurity technologies, such technologies must be securely configured. In our reviews of cybersecurity controls at federal agencies, we have found several instances where the effectiveness of technology was limited because it was improperly configured.[44] For example, failing to remove default passwords that are commonly known can lead to the exploitation of vulnerabilities, resulting in compromised computers and networks.

The effectiveness of various technologies, including firewalls and intrusion detection systems, is highly dependent on proper configuration. To illustrate, deploying a firewall with its "out-of-the-box" security settings may be equivalent to installing a steel door, yet leaving it wide open. The firewall must be properly configured to effectively implement the agency's policies and procedures.

There are a number of federal sources for guidance on the configurations of several of these technologies. As discussed above, NIST is required to develop checklists to assist agencies in configuring technologies. In addition, the Defense Information Systems Agency (DISA) and NSA have prepared implementation guides to help their administrators configure their systems in a secure manner.[45] In configuring technologies, it is important to consider this and other available guidance, adapting it as necessary to reflect the particular circumstances of its implementation.

As agreed with your offices, unless you publicly announce the contents of the report earlier, we plan no further distribution until 30 days from the report date. At that time, we will send copies of this report to the Ranking Minority Members of the Committee on Government Reform and the Subcommittee on Technology, Information Policy, Intergovernmental Relations, and the Census and other interested parties. In addition, the report will be made available at no charge on GAO's Web site at http://www.gao.gov.

---

[44]U.S. General Accounting Office, *Information Security: Fundamental Weaknesses Place EPA Data and Operations at Risk,* GAO/AIMD-00-215 (Washington, D.C.: July 6, 2000); *Information Security: Weaknesses Place Commerce Data and Operations at Serious Risk,* GAO-01-751 (Washington, D.C.: August 13, 2001); *FDIC Information Security: Improvements Made but Weaknesses Remain,* GAO-02-689 (Washington, D.C.: July 15, 2002); *FDIC Information Security: Progress Made but Existing Weaknesses Place Data at Risk,* GAO-03-630 (Washington, D.C.: June 18, 2003); and *Information Security: Computer Controls over Key Treasury Internet Payment System,* GAO-03-837 (Washington, D.C.: July 30, 2003).

[45]For DISA's security technical implementation guides, see http://csrc.nist.gov/pcig/cig.html. For NSA's security recommendation guides, see http://www.nsa.gov/snac/index.html.

If you have any questions regarding this report, please contact Robert Dacey at (202) 512-3317, Keith Rhodes at (202) 512-6412, or Elizabeth Johnston, Assistant Director, at (202) 512-6345. We can also be reached by e-mail at daceyr@gao.gov, rhodesk@gao.gov, and johnstone@gao.gov respectively. Key contributors to this report are listed in appendix II.

Robert F. Dacey
Director, Information Security Issues

Keith A. Rhodes
Chief Technologist

Appendix I: Objective, Scope, and Methodology

Our objective was to identify commercially available, state-of-the-practice cybersecurity technologies that federal agencies can use to secure their computer systems. To gather information on available tools and products, we conducted an extensive literature search and obtained and perused technical reports from government and independent organizations, articles in technical magazines, market analyses, and vendor-provided information. We discussed aspects of newer technologies with industry representatives at a major government security exposition and conference where these technologies were demonstrated.

To organize the information we collected for our catalog, we researched existing frameworks for describing cybersecurity technologies that have been developed by other federal agencies, industry groups, and independent organizations.[1] Using this information, we developed a taxonomy that categorizes technologies according to the functionality they provide and then specifies types within those categories. However, there is a plethora of cybersecurity products and tools on the market, many of which provide a range of functions. Moreover, the marketplace is dynamic: New products are constantly being introduced, and general-purpose products often integrate the functionalities of special-purpose tools once they have been proven useful. Consequently, we recognize that this

---

[1]NIST's *Guide to Selecting Information Technology Security Products* discusses security products according to the following categories: identification and authentication, access control, intrusion detection, firewall, public key infrastructure, and malicious code protection. The Institute for Information Infrastructure Protection, in its *National Information Infrastructure Protection Research and Development Agenda Initiative Report,* groups security cybersecurity technologies into the following categories: audit and post-event analysis, authorization/access control, boundary protection, cryptographic controls, identification and authentication, integrity protection, intrusion/anomaly detection, nonrepudiation and related controls, secure configuration management and assurance, security administration, and secure backup/recovery/reconstitution.

taxonomy is neither exhaustive nor perfect. Nevertheless, it does provide a framework for grouping and discussing the most pervasive technologies we discovered in our research. Finally, we relied on previous GAO work on information technology security. We performed our work from June 2003 through February 2004.

Appendix II: Staff Acknowledgments

Acknowledgments

Key contributors to this report were Edward Alexander Jr., Scott Borre, Lon Chin, Joanne Fiorino, Richard Hung, Elizabeth Johnston, Christopher Kovach, Anjalique Lawrence, Min Lee, Stephanie Lee, and Tracy Pierson.

| GAO's Mission | The General Accounting Office, the audit, evaluation and investigative arm of Congress, exists to support Congress in meeting its constitutional responsibilities and to help improve the performance and accountability of the federal government for the American people. GAO examines the use of public funds; evaluates federal programs and policies; and provides analyses, recommendations, and other assistance to help Congress make informed oversight, policy, and funding decisions. GAO's commitment to good government is reflected in its core values of accountability, integrity, and reliability. |

| Obtaining Copies of GAO Reports and Testimony | The fastest and easiest way to obtain copies of GAO documents at no cost is through the Internet. GAO's Web site (www.gao.gov) contains abstracts and full-text files of current reports and testimony and an expanding archive of older products. The Web site features a search engine to help you locate documents using key words and phrases. You can print these documents in their entirety, including charts and other graphics.

Each day, GAO issues a list of newly released reports, testimony, and correspondence. GAO posts this list, known as "Today's Reports," on its Web site daily. The list contains links to the full-text document files. To have GAO e-mail this list to you every afternoon, go to www.gao.gov and select "Subscribe to e-mail alerts" under the "Order GAO Products" heading. |

| Order by Mail or Phone | The first copy of each printed report is free. Additional copies are $2 each. A check or money order should be made out to the Superintendent of Documents. GAO also accepts VISA and Mastercard. Orders for 100 or more copies mailed to a single address are discounted 25 percent. Orders should be sent to:

U.S. General Accounting Office
441 G Street NW, Room LM
Washington, D.C. 20548

To order by Phone: Voice: (202) 512-6000
                     TDD: (202) 512-2537
                     Fax: (202) 512-6061 |

| To Report Fraud, Waste, and Abuse in Federal Programs | Contact:

Web site: www.gao.gov/fraudnet/fraudnet.htm
E-mail: fraudnet@gao.gov
Automated answering system: (800) 424-5454 or (202) 512-7470 |

| Public Affairs | Jeff Nelligan, Managing Director, NelliganJ@gao.gov (202) 512-4800
U.S. General Accounting Office, 441 G Street NW, Room 7149
Washington, D.C. 20548 |